FORTNITE

OUTFITS 2
COLLECTORS' EDITION

CONTENTS

OUTFITS AND SETS

LOOKING FOR A PARTICULAR GEAR SET? HERE'S WHERE TO FIND ALL OF THE OUTFITS AND OTHER ITEMS FEATURED IN THIS BOOK!

FEATURES

AWESOME OUTFITS

FORTNITE FASHION IS AN ESSENTIAL PART OF YOUR BATTLE ROYALE EXPERIENCE

The Outfit you rock makes a big statement. Choosing to drop from the Battle Bus dressed like a dark destroyer, a mysterious menace, or a half-peeled banana says a lot about the type of player you are. Earning a Victory Royale is the ultimate aim, but doing it in style with an impressive look is even better!

In addition to selecting the Outfit that best represents you, you can also choose from a range of cool cosmetic items, including Back Bling, Harvesting Tools, Gliders, and Pets. Your style can be a clever combination from your favorite sets, or simply go with the flow and sport the full look from a single set.

This book showcases some of the most exciting new looks that have appeared in the latest seasons, arranged by sets for easy reference. Get ready for a Fortnite fashion festival and pick up some top stats and facts about the slickest Outfits in the game.

GET THE LOOK

Fortnite is played in third person mode, with your character always in your view, so of course you want to keep them looking fresh, fun... or fearsome! Some players target a look that's pure warrior, showing off a battle-ready Outfit that will get the enemy's heartbeat racing. Others prefer a more relaxed and casual dress style that's more laidback than lethal. There are no right or wrong choices—flex in the Fortnite fashion and vibe that most grabs you.

SET IT OUT, OR STYLE IT OUT

Fortnite makes it easy for you to rock a certain theme or look. Sets can include an Outfit plus Back Bling, Harvesting Tool, Glider and even Wraps that are all designed to reflect and complement the theme of the collection. There's nothing stopping you from mixing and matching different Outfits, though, if you want to be unique and individual with your wardrobe.

VISIT THE STORE

Ideas for Outfits can come from watching popular streamers in action, other players in your squad, and also the Item Shop. Cool new cosmetics cycle into the Item Shop every day, which can be bought with V-Bucks or, if you're lucky, gifted to you from other players. It's a great place to see all the latest Outfits and sets, so make sure you visit regularly to browse new stuff.

FAST-PACED FORTNITE

Fortnite is a fast-moving world of adventures, events, characters, and seasons—that's what keeps it fresh! There's always something to amaze and intrigue you, including new items, maps, and rewards for completing Battle Pass tiers. Fortnite just never stands still!

AEROSOL ASSASSINS

TAG ALONG AND TAKE DOWN THE OPPOSITION

STREET SHINE

KOMPLEX

INTRODUCED IN:
CHAPTER 2: SEASON 2
RARITY: RARE

Aerosol Assassins is a busy set, with four Outfits by Chapter 2: Season 2, and Komplex is well worthy of inclusion. Catching the eye in the Item Shop, her subtle paint splats don't distract from her overall chilling-but-chilled-out vibe. Komplex could be earned ahead of release by participating in the Australian Summer Splash Cup.

TILTED TEKNIQUE

INTRODUCED IN: SEASON X
RARITY: EPIC

Back in Season 4, the Aerosol Assassins set showed off the debut Teknique Outfit, along with her spray-painting buddy Abstrakt. In Season X, Tilted Teknique joined the ranks and she takes the look to a fresh new level. Available at Tier 20 of the Battle Pass, the mean black Outfit is splashed with bright paint on the ripped pants, gloves, and hoodie.

Being a progressive Outfit, Tilted Teknique revealed further variants as you attained higher levels—reach Tier 23 and the hoodie is dropped for a black top emblazoned with the Tilted logo. Completing the Battle Pass' Spray and Pray mission unlocked the white Streetstyle, while the orange Wildstyle appeared after the Prestige Blockbuster mission was ticked off.

RENEGADE ROLLERS

AIR ROYALE
HIT MACH SPEED AND LET BATTLE COMMENCE

SUPERSONIC

INTRODUCED IN: SEASON 8
RARITY: LEGENDARY

The Supersonic Outfit flew into Fortnite just in time for the Air Royale Limited Time Mode, so it made sense to name this set after the Season 8 LTM. The jetfighter pilot suit has a fearsome skull marked on the helmet and a menacing black aviation look that's enough to make the opposition shake in their flying boots. As well as the Skull variant, there's also the Hornet, Falcon, and Wolf style in the Supersonic bundle, but one of the most unique things about this entire Outfit is the Gauge Back Bling. It has a "real-time" LED display that shows the number of eliminations you have racked up in that match.

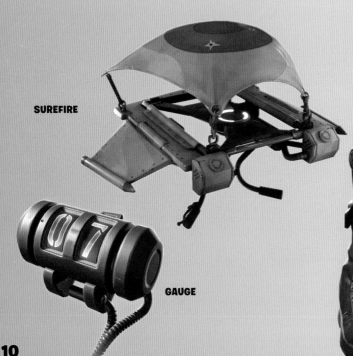

SUREFIRE

GAUGE

FACT

The Air Royale loading screen was unlockable via reaching Tier 50 of the Season 9 Battle Pass, showing an action-packed aerial image of planes and players battling in the sky!

HEMLOCK

INTRODUCED IN: CHAPTER 2: SEASON 1
RARITY: EPIC

The Fortnitemares event unmasked this frightening Outfit and shook up the Halloween scene. The default style was spooky enough with its green hair, red eyes, and pale skin, but the selectable option unmasked a monster Outfit with razor-sharp teeth and haunting features. Only a black cat and a broomstick could add extra edge to this ghoulish gear.

SPELLSLINGER

DELIRIUM

INTRODUCED IN: CHAPTER 2: SEASON 1
RARITY: EPIC

Is this Outfit really an illusion? Face Delirium on the map and you'll soon see how genuine he is. The hooded menace is definitely a scary dude and no one dares to take a close-up look at what's lurking behind those evil and enigmatic eyes.

ASCENSION
RISE UP TO THE CHALLENGE

JOURNEY VS HAZARD

INTRODUCED IN:
CHAPTER 2: SEASON 1
RARITY: RARE

Red is traditionally the color of danger, but you're advised to "think pink" and watch out for the havoc that Journey vs Danger can create. Another selectable style in Chapter 2's debut season Battle Pass, Journey, was unlocked at Tier 1 and was soon followed by the darker and more mysterious Hazard. The Base Jumper Glider gets Journey vs Hazard on the path to chasing a Victory Royale.

BOULDER BREAKERS

BASECAMP BAG

BAD MEDICINE
MED SUPPLIES ARE ON THE WAY

REMEDY VS TOXIN

INTRODUCED IN: CHAPTER 2: SEASON 1
RARITY: RARE

The Chapter 2: Season 1 Battle Pass was full of selectable style Outfits, always a popular choice. Reaching Tier 40 unlocked Remedy and unleashed a street-smart medic in funky pants and jacket, complete with cap to show her "friendly" intentions. This is the A.L.T.E.R. part of the Outfit, with the E.G.O. arriving in the more sinister-looking Toxin once further missions were completed. Toxin's evil green getup marks her out as someone to keep a close eye on.

MEDAXE

ANTIDOTE

FACT

A cool purple style of Remedy vs Toxin could be unlocked through the Alter Ego Challenges during Chapter 2: Season 1.

BANANA BUNCH
IT'S TIME TO GO BANANAS

PEELY

INTRODUCED IN: SEASON 8
RARITY: EPIC

The classic Tomatohead Outfit from Season 3 showed that fruit and Fortnite are a winning mixture, so Peely's arrival was always going to create a stir. Strutting around the island in a banana Outfit will bring a smile to anyone's face, which is why this cosmetic was one of the highlights of the Season 8 Battle Pass, with Peely unlocked at Tier 47.

Peely is fun looking and even has a wacky fruit sticker on the back, but don't be fooled as this Outfit means serious business, too. Go for this and it will be quite the game changer—Peely is reactive and starts with a green shade before ripening to bright yellow and will develop ripe spots as a match continues.

PEELY PICK

FACT
The first Fortnite reactive Outfit was the Legendary Deadfire in Season 6.

BANANA ROYALE
QUICK, LET'S SPLIT

AGENT PEELY

INTRODUCED IN:
CHAPTER 2: SEASON 2
RARITY: EPIC

Secret agents descended onto the map when the Chapter 2: Season 2 Battle Pass arrived. Any gamers who didn't get involved will be kicking themselves now, because Agent Peely is a super-cool character. Standing out from the regular Peely Outfit thanks to his sunglass-shaped eyes, mega-moody demeanor and bow tie with tweed suit, this operative can handle any mission he's assigned. Peel away the layers and, just like for most of the Battle Pass Outfits, there are unlockable styles of Ghost and Shadow, plus the Golden Agent, which were revealed the further you got through the challenges.

BANANA BRIEFCASE

BANANAXE

FACT

Chapter 2: Season 2 Battle Pass players could choose between the Ghost or Shadow factions, with the Outfit variants taking on a pale or dark style depending on your pick.

BANNER BRIGADE
KEEPING COLORFUL COMPANY

BANNER CAPE

SGT. SIGIL

INTRODUCED IN: SEASON 9
RARITY: UNCOMMON

Combat trousers and chunky laced-up boots, matched with a bright yellow sports tee and cap, says that Sgt. Sigil is a simple but determined character. As part of the Banner Brigade set that features many similar-looking colorful and sporty Outfits, she comes from a team that's used to winning, so don't mess.

BANNER SHIELD

SIGNATURE SNIPER

INTRODUCED IN: SEASON 9
RARITY: UNCOMMON

This guy is pretty sure of himself—a goatee, mustache, long hair, reversed cap, and neon shirt is not a look for the meek and mild. Signature Sniper hits the spot for players who want an athletic look but aren't afraid to stand out from the crowd, because this eye-catching gear won't go unnoticed.

BATTLE DYNAMICS
MECHANICAL FAILURE IS NOT ACCEPTABLE AS A NEW ERA RISES

HOT WING

SENTINEL

INTRODUCED IN: SEASON 9
RARITY: LEGENDARY

Far from just keeping watch and hanging back in battle, this rooster soldier also has the mechanical skills and power to take it right to the enemy and deal with dangerous situations. Starting with the head, Sentinel may look like a classic Roman guard (albeit with a beak) but there's nothing outdated about this Outfit, and its imposing presence is certain to cause your foes to chicken out of a confrontation. Collect the Hot Wing Back Bling to complete a soldier that's as advanced—and wild—as you can imagine.

FACT

Sentinel was a Tier 1 reward in the Season 9 Battle Pass, but for determined players the Dark selectable variant was unlocked at Tier 99.

BEACH BATTALION
HEAD FOR THE SAND AND SEE WHAT'S ROCKING

LAGUNA

INTRODUCED IN: CHAPTER 8
RARITY: RARE

Outfits that are part of a Pack always get pulses racing, because they're much rarer than those in the Item Shop or Battle Pass. The Laguna Pack introduced Fortnite fans to this fresh Outfit, which draws on sandy beach vibes with a dose of pineapple goodness thrown in for good measure. The Pineapple Strummer Back Bling creates a relaxed look to Laguna and using the Pineapple Wrap means you can add a fruity feel to your weapons as well.

FACT
The Laguna Pack was the first to come with a wrap as part of the package. The extra benefit included was the popular Pineapple Wrap.

MARINO

INTRODUCED IN: CHAPTER 8
RARITY: RARE

Beach hat, orange-tinted shades, and flower-patterned shirt suggest Marino is totally ready for a fun trip to the beach. He can take care of business around the island first, though, and with three bananas strapped on his Banana Bag Back Bling, he has plenty of food to keep his energy levels topped up.

BEAR BRIGADE
ICE TO SEE YOU, FOLKS

POLAR PATROLLER

INTRODUCED IN:
CHAPTER 2: SEASON 1
RARITY: EPIC

Polar bears are a protected animal, and this animal looks very capable of protecting his squad in a tense tussle. A bruising bulk of a bear, Polar Patroller is one of the mightiest characters and not an opponent you want to face up to without a plan of how to take it down. It's difficult to imagine Polar Patroller's scary snarl ever changing to a smile and, even with one eye, this creature will scan the landscape to quickly deal with danger.

ICE FISHER

BONE BRIGADE
CHILL TO THE BONE

SKLAXIS

INTRODUCED IN: CHAPTER 2: SEASON 1
RARITY: EPIC

Ssssscary alert! Sklaxis arrived in the Item Shop in Chapter 2: Season 1 and caused a stir as a human-like reptile, showing off a hissing green tongue and eyes that light up and flicker around the sides of its hood. Sklaxis' "face" is carved from a bony material that also makes up spiky arm and shoulder plates. This dude is a wiry and slithery customer that's as difficult to predict as its name is to pronounce.

FACT
Sklaxis has a close resemblance to the creepy Cloaked Star Outfit from Season 5, but the pair are not related.

BOUNTY HUNTER
SEARCH AND DESTROY IS WHAT IT'S ALL ABOUT

VEGA

INTRODUCED IN: SEASON 9
RARITY: EPIC

Hunting is a specialty for Vega. Season 9 saw the introduction of the Fortbytes collectible items for Battle Pass owners, and the Vega Outfit needed to be unlocked at Tier 47 so that the Fortbyte #19 location could be discovered. The Go Bag Back Bling finishes off this compact but fearless Outfit. It also has two selectable styles with contrasting colors that could be achieved when missions were finished as part of the Vega Challenges.

REVOKER

GO BAG

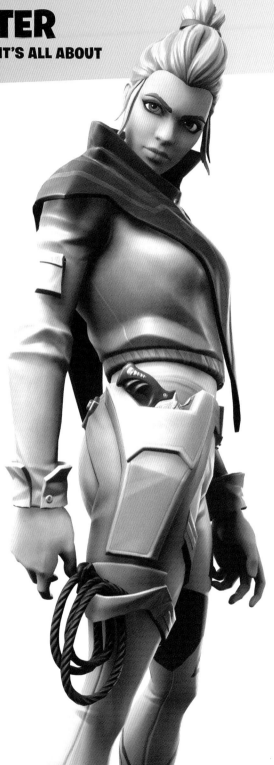

BROKEN LIGHT

WAKE UP TO A NIGHTMARE

ARCANA

SHATTERED WING

DREAM

INTRODUCED IN: SEASON 8
RARITY: RARE

Sometimes your Fortnite dreams can come true! In Season 8, Dream entered the Item Shop and players moved quickly to get this gear in their locker. Purple and pink is the theme, which manages to make both a friendly and frightening-looking Outfit at the same time. Study the eyes and you'll see they are a piercing light blue. The Broken Light Set includes the awesome Arcana Glider, Shattered Wing Back Bling, and Shard Break Wrap—score all four and opponents will be having sleepless nights.

BROOD
LOOK INTO MY EYES

HYBRID

INTRODUCED IN: SEASON 8
RARITY: LEGENDARY

When sets like Brood and Outfits as desirable as Hybrid come along, Battle Pass holders can really begin to get excited. Tier 1 of Season 8 was rewarded with the Legendary Outfit Hybrid, who is a burnt orange ninja with skills spilling out of every crease of the armor. The selectable styles from the Hybrid Challenges saw stacks of variants follow, including progressive Outfits featuring dragon-like ninjas and blue, black, and ultraviolet-themed warriors.

FACT

Even when a season is over, XP earned in the future still counts towards completing a challenge from that season and unlocking progressive Outfits.

DRAGON'S
CLAW

27

BRUTE FORCE
XL SIZE DELIVERS XL POWER

HACK & SMASH

HENCH HAULER

BRUTUS

INTRODUCED IN: CHAPTER 2: SEASON 2
RARITY: EPIC

If you're stuck in a dark alley with this fella, there will be a couple of problems. First, he's a terrifying opponent up close, and second, you'll never squeeze past Brutus in a tight spot! Part of the exciting secret agent-themed Battle Pass, this hulking hero was unlocked at Tier 20, with the masked Ghost and Shadow variants coming into play through the Brutus' Briefing Challenges. Brutus is also an enlightened Outfit, as past Tier 140 he'll start to change and take on his Golden Agent persona. Powerful and colorful—a winning combination.

FACT

The final Brutus' Briefing mission before selecting your Shadow or Ghost variant was to steal security plans from The Rig, The Shark, or The Yacht and deliver them to your selected faction.

B.R.U.T.E. SQUAD
FEEL THE B.R.U.T.E. FORCE

B.R.U.T.E. GUNNER

INTRODUCED IN: SEASON X
RARITY: UNCOMMON

Sleek, powerful, and mysterious are three great words to sum up this Season X Outfit. The two-tone black cosmetic is durable but flexible, with reinforced padding around the arms, legs, and shoulders just in case things get tough. B.R.U.T.E. Gunner's helmet is part motorcyclist and part futuristic flyer—that visor shields one cool-looking lady.

B.R.U.T.E. NAVIGATOR

INTRODUCED IN: SEASON X
RARITY: UNCOMMON

Slightly stockier than B.R.U.T.E. Gunner, B.R.U.T.E. Navigator comes ready-made for a Battle Royale that requires stealth, speed, and style. The Outfit combines a strong superhero-type look with a touch of swagger that can leave opponents baffled by what his next move will be. Team it with the Robo Wrecker Harvesting Tool to complete the dynamic pose.

CRYPTIC
BECOME THE MASTER OF MYSTERY

SPECTURAL SPINE

CRYPTIC

INTRODUCED IN: SEASON 9
RARITY: RARE

Ultra modern and ultra hip, Cryptic kicks out neon splashes and moody black clothing to totally master a look that's both chilled and chilling to face. The shoes, pants, body warmer, shirt, and gloves have flashes of bright color, matching the haunting yellow eyes lurking underneath Cryptic's sporty cap. This guy's Spectral Spine Back Bling, which floats and glows, adds to his empowering mysteriousness.

FACT

The Cryptic set comes with the animated Enigma wrap which looks epic when it creates a holographic-like ripple effect on weapons.

CUSTOM
CHOOSE A UNIQUE PATH

GEAR SPECIALIST MAYA

INTRODUCED IN: CHAPTER 2: SEASON 2
RARITY: LEGENDARY

The Chapter 2: Season 2 Battle Pass opened the door to Shadow and Ghost secret agent Outfits, as well as another memorable first. Gear Specialist Maya became the original customizable Outfit—her hair, tattoos, boots, pants, vests, colors, face paints, and much more could all be selected to suit your own taste. Building her visual options was possible as you progressed through the challenges, which gave you extra incentives to beat the missions and spend time creating your unique cosmetic. Players had to remember to actually leave some time free to join in a Battle Royale too, though...

ARROYO PACK

SPECIALIST PICKAXE

CUSTOM FLIER

FACT

A mind-boggling 3.8 million combinations of different customizable options could be selected with Gear Specialist Maya!

DIABOLICAL
YOU'RE GONNA GET FIRED

DOMINION

INTRODUCED IN:
CHAPTER 2: SEASON 1
RARITY: EPIC

From head to toe, Dominion has a burning desire to be the best and grab a Victory Royale. His flame-soled boots give him a demonic touch that licks up throughout the rest of his gear, while the Flame Sigil Back Bling looks super "hot" and appears as if it would keep burning even in a snowstorm.

BURNING BEAST

BURNING AXE

FACT

The Diabolical set also featured the Legendary Malice Outfit, Dominion's red-hot female equivalent, in Season 8.

DINO GUARD

COME AND JOIN THE PREHISTORIC PARTY

BRONTO

INTRODUCED IN: SEASON X
RARITY: RARE

Coming from the same set as the classic Rex and Tricera Ops, Bronto had much to live up to when he arrived in the Item Shop in Season X. Luckily, this dino-themed dude didn't bite off more than he could chew and delivered another fan favorite Outfit that brings the prehistoric right up to date!

BRONTO BAG

DOMINATION
WEAKNESS DOES NOT EXIST

PLASMATIC EDGE

OPPRESSOR

INTRODUCED IN: SEASON X
RARITY: LEGENDARY

From every angle, Oppressor just looks monstrously bad (in a good way, that is) and not the type you want to get on the wrong side of. The mechanical menace caught eyes in the Item Shop in Season X, along with the Domination set's Exo-Spine Back Bling, and the selectable blue style only ramped up the demand for this Legendary Outfit.

EXO-SPINE

FACT

Look closely at Oppressor's chest and forearms and you'll see mysterious lines and markings. Maybe these count the enemies it has taken down?

DRIFT
KEEP MOVING AND KEEP GROOVING

ATMOSPHERE

DUAL EDGE

KITSUNE

CATALYST

INTRODUCED IN: SEASON X
RARITY: LEGENDARY

Fans of the original Drift Outfit from Season 5 could not wait to jump into the Battle Pass for Season X. Rocking the same street-savvy vibe, Catalyst was obtained from Tier 1 and her punky, no-nonsense Outfit once again proved a hit just like Drift did. Five variants could be obtained after further progress through the Battle Pass, including Hoodie, Overcoat, and Overcharged. Riftstorm and Snowstorm were available as mission-based rewards and swapped Catalyst's black and purple scheme for silver-gray and white.

FACT

Several vehicle tasks were part of the Road Trip Prestige Challenges to unlock the Riftstorm style, such as eliminations while riding a vehicle.

FALCON CLAN
KEEPING THE COMPETITION UNDER WRAPS

KENJI

INTRODUCED IN: SEASON 8
RARITY: EPIC

FALCON

Swooping into the Item Shop in Season 8, Kenji and Kuno showed that the Falcon Clan set was ready to hunt some prey. Clearly inspired by the ancient Asian artistry of kung fu warriors, this male and female pair look like they don't take any prisoners. Kenji is actually sporting baggy shorts, but he's not on a leisurely vacation and his bandaged legs, arms, and face are more for show and suspense than to hide any weaknesses. The silver-streaked ponytail keeps his flowing locks out of his face, and although one eye is out of action, Kenji himself needs watching closely at all times.

TALONS

KUNO

INTRODUCED IN: SEASON 8
RARITY: EPIC

Kuno looks like she could be related to Kenji as she rocks the same hair color and style, with casual combat gear and more bandages than can be found in a doctor's surgery. Her face is partially covered, adding to the mystique around her persona, but there's no disguising the fact this is an Outfit well worth seeking out. Finally, what makes Kuno and Kenji even more in demand is when they are matched with the Falcon Glider—the sound of this big bird screeching as it drops onto the island is unmistakable.

FARM STAND
EARNING YOUR CORN COMES AT A PRICE

**POWER
PITCH**

FARMER STEEL

INTRODUCED IN: CHAPTER 2: SEASON 2
RARITY: RARE

Don't ever accuse him of being just an aging
field worker who doesn't know how to handle
himself in battle. Sure, Farmer Steel is old
school, but he's used to the cut and thrust
of island combat and if you stray into his
area, he'll harvest you quicker than you can
say "breakfast cereal." So don't be fooled by
the tattered hat and white beard, because
experience is always a worthwhile weapon.

**HEAVY
HARVESTER**

FATHOMS DEEP
EVEN IN THE WATER, YOU CAN STILL SOLDIER ON

DEPTH CHARGER

BULL SHARK

INTRODUCED IN: CHAPTER 2: SEASON 1
RARITY: RARE

Remember Chomp Sr. from Season 5? He's all shark teeth and fins, which is also the look that Bull Shark is going for, except his gleaming white choppers are painted onto his hood in an Outfit that's part ocean diver and part soldier. Included in the Fathoms Deep set, Bull Shark definitely doesn't look out of his depth.

MANTA

STINGRAY

INTRODUCED IN: CHAPTER 2: SEASON 1
RARITY: RARE

Woah, what a look! Stingray is decked in regular skinny pants with a sporty active shirt and short-sleeved jacket, however it's all totally dominated by the incredible headgear. Caught in some kind of super-strength black fishing net that masks glowing eyes, there's no doubting that Stingray achieves an appearance quite unlike any other on land or water.

SEA SCORPION

TRENCH RAIDER

INTRODUCED IN: CHAPTER 2: SEASON 1
RARITY: RARE

Trench Raider has the aura of a military man that could take on any mission. His suit reflects a practical and professional approach—all dark patches and carefully crafted protective panels—and he looks like he spends a good 15 minutes styling his hair each morning. Let's not quibble on details, though, as Trench Raider will totally have your squad's back in a tense tussle with the opposition. At ease, soldier.

GREAT GLIDERS

FALL WITH TOTAL STYLE AND LET GAMERS KNOW YOU MEAN BUSINESS

The moment you drop from the Battle Bus, you have the option to deploy your Glider and make your first statement in a match. The type of flyer you use says much about your character. Either drop down with a stealth-like Glider, burst onto the scene with something eye-catching or use a classic Umbrella to let others know who's the boss. There are stacks to choose, and here are just some of Fortnite's coolest Gliders ever...

BOMBS AWAY!

INTRODUCED IN:
CHAPTER 2: SEASON 2
RARITY: EPIC

What an explosive Battle Pass Glider! Bombs Away! is the first that can be ridden while standing on top of it, plus it has two selectable styles based on which faction you choose.

BURNING BEAST

INTRODUCED IN:
CHAPTER 2: SEASON 1
RARITY: LEGENDARY

Coming from the red-hot Diabolical set, swooping down with this flaming creature could set you off to a blazing start.

CUDDLE CRUISER

INTRODUCED IN: SEASON 8
RARITY: RARE

Matching the Cuddle Team Leader Outfit with this cute Glider really gets the most out of the Royale Hearts set—the enemy will not bear it!

SKY SERPENTS

INTRODUCED IN: SEASON 8
RARITY: RARE

These sssscary snakes spell double trouble as you land and definitely do not send the message that you'd like to make friends.

TURBO SPIN

INTRODUCED IN: SEASON 9
RARITY: EPIC

Unlocked at Tier 15 of the Battle Pass, the engines and giant wingspan on Turbo Spin give it the look of a pure futuristic spacecraft.

STUNT CYCLE

INTRODUCED IN: SEASON X
RARITY: RARE

Gliders come in all shapes and sizes, and the shape of Stunt Cycle is unmistakably a mean motorbike converted into a crazy gliding machine. Nice.

SPRAY SAIL

INTRODUCED IN: SEASON X
RARITY: EPIC

Just a piece of scrap iron, this Glider's party trick is the cool spray can that appears to magically paint a colorful design.

SKY STRIPE

INTRODUCED IN: SEASON X
RARITY: UNCOMMON

Simple but effective, Sky Stripe gets you to the ground with minimal fuss. Less is more with a straightforward Glider like this one.

ASSAULT BOMBER

INTRODUCED IN: SEASON 9
RARITY: EPIC

Why glide when you can fly? Get the feeling of flying from the Battle Bus with a Glider that mimics a bomber plane. Prepare for landing!

WILD BLAST

INTRODUCED IN:
CHAPTER 2: SEASON 2
RARITY: UNCOMMON

Colorful, crazy shapes, wings, and a canopy—Wild Blast packs a lot of character and style into its explosive design.

STEELWING

INTRODUCED IN: SEASON X
RARITY: LEGENDARY

It's hard work unlocking this tough Glider, because you need to reach Tier 95 of the Battle Pass. Well worth the effort, though.

CLASSIFIED

INTRODUCED IN:
CHAPTER 2: SEASON 2
RARITY: UNCOMMON

Claim a Victory Royale and this gold and black glitzy Umbrella was all yours in Chapter 2: Season 2. We salute you!

RETALIATOR

INTRODUCED IN: SEASON 9
RARITY: RARE

Designed to perfectly match the Vendetta Outfit, Retaliator gives any player an air of robotic ruthlessness.

CHOPPA

INTRODUCED IN: SEASON 8
RARITY: EPIC

Need some air support? Call in the troops with this slick machine from the awesome Tropic Troopers set.

PIXEL PILOT

INTRODUCED IN: SEASON X
RARITY: RARE

Another Battle Pass favourite, it's a retro arcade machine with selectable red and blue variants for a proper gaming blast from the past!

OLLIE

INTRODUCED IN:
CHAPTER 2: SEASON 2
RARITY: EPIC

Reach Tier 64 of the Battle Bass and this cute but creepy creation can be equipped as you float to the island. Selectable styles of Ghost and Shadow.

MAN O' WAR

INTRODUCED IN: SEASON 9
RARITY: EPIC

Think something fishy is going on? It will be after you drop from the Battle Bus attached to this special sea-based spectacle!

HOME RUN

INTRODUCED IN: SEASON 8
RARITY: UNCOMMON

Hit the opposition out of the ballpark as you swoop down with the Home Run Glider, part of the baseball-themed Three Strikes set.

FINAL RECKONING

LOSERS NEVER GET A LAST CHANCE

CHAOS
SCYTHE

OOZE CHAMBER

CHAOS AGENT

INTRODUCED IN: CHAPTER 2: SEASON 1
RARITY: EPIC

Not much was known about the E.G.O. and A.L.T.E.R. groups when they appeared in Chapter 2: Season 1. These mysterious organizations contain key characters, of which Chaos Agent is a leading figure of A.L.T.E.R. With an instantly recognizable appearance of masked hood, bugged-out eyes, and three-fingered gloves, this slimline Outfit is still a heavyweight style that proves popular again and again in the Item Shop.

FACT

The selectable style for Chaos Agent is Goopy, which replaces the mask with a black sludge that wafts away from the head and left shoulder.

GOO GLIDER

JAWBREAKER

INTRODUCED IN: CHAPTER 2: SEASON 1
RARITY: RARE

Final Reckoning is a busy set, full of Outfits, Gliders, Harvesting Tools, and Wraps. For such a hectic collection, Jawbreaker is refreshingly calm and stylish with a black and dark gray theme carried through the camo shorts, thigh-high socks, and cropped top. Even Jawbreaker's shades match the outfit and the dark tattoos on her forearms finish off a powerful but self-possessed presence.

TEEF

INTRODUCED IN:
CHAPTER 2: SEASON 1
RARITY: EPIC

GLOBBER

Sometimes, an Outfit's name just sums up their appearance perfectly, with very little else needed to be added. Teef is one of those, because this dude's mighty mouth dominates to a degree achieved by very few others. Coupled with the equally bonkers Nosh Back Bling and Goo Glider, this Outfit offers Fortnite players a fearsome combination and that's the whole tooth—sorry, "truth."

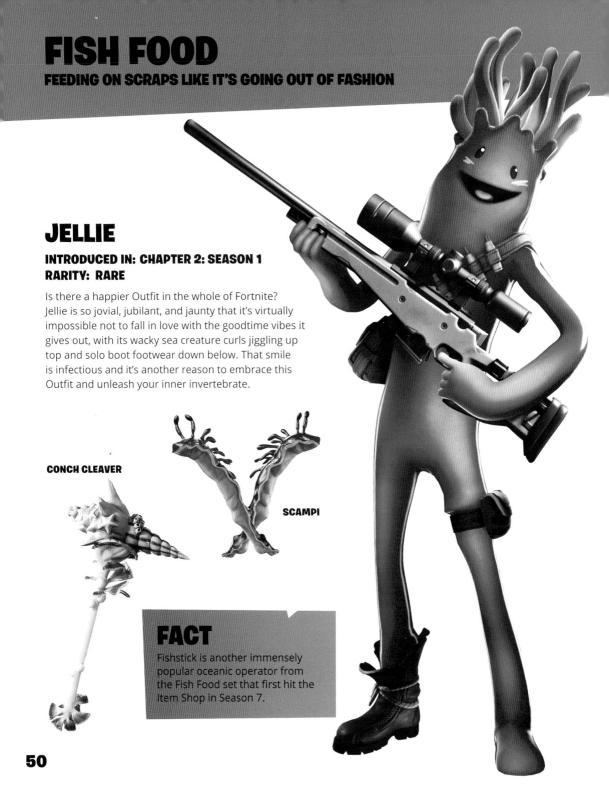

FISH FOOD
FEEDING ON SCRAPS LIKE IT'S GOING OUT OF FASHION

JELLIE

INTRODUCED IN: CHAPTER 2: SEASON 1
RARITY: RARE

Is there a happier Outfit in the whole of Fortnite? Jellie is so jovial, jubilant, and jaunty that it's virtually impossible not to fall in love with the goodtime vibes it gives out, with its wacky sea creature curls jiggling up top and solo boot footwear down below. That smile is infectious and it's another reason to embrace this Outfit and unleash your inner invertebrate.

CONCH CLEAVER

SCAMPI

FACT

Fishstick is another immensely popular oceanic operator from the Fish Food set that first hit the Item Shop in Season 7.

STARFISH

INTRODUCED IN: SEASON 9
RARITY: EPIC

From the shoulders up, Starfish presents regular human-like features with just a few hints of amphibian awesomeness in her eyes and in those curious curves on her head. Look below the shoulders, though, and the fishy clues stack up... it's all scaly limbs and webbed appendages that make this Outfit a must-have for land and sea battles.

SHELLIE

TRIGGERFISH

INTRODUCED IN: CHAPTER 2: SEASON 1
RARITY: RARE

Taking the Fishstick Outfit to a new level of uniqueness isn't easy, but Triggerfish does it without breaking sweat... not that fish can sweat, of course. Anyway, this warrior adds moody combat face paint to its bulging bright orange head and dons mean military clothes as a sign that the competition should swim for their lives. Three variants can be selected—with and without face paint and a telescopic helmet—to get gamers even more hooked on the Outfit.

FORT KNIGHTS
IT'S TIME TO GET MEDIEVAL

ULTIMA KNIGHT

INTRODUCED IN: SEASON X
RARITY: LEGENDARY

Ultima Knight is linked to a long list of past season legends and needs to show the strength and tenacity of such imposing Outfits as Black Knight, Royale Knight, and Red Knight from this set. Luckily, Ultima Knight has the skillset to match those armor-clad figures—indeed players only got their hands on him if they achieved Tier 100 of the Season X Battle Pass. Red and silver variants were unlocked after further missions were completed—if you see any of these in a battle with you, then it could be time to say good-knight!

DRAGONCREST

FACT

Fort Knights is one of the oldest and most revered sets in Fortnite, having first appeared in Season 2. Show some respect to these ancient warriors!

SPARKLE SUPREME

INTRODUCED IN: SEASON X
RARITY: EPIC

The Sparkle Specialist Outfit lit up the battlefield in Season 2, then Sparkle Supreme arrived on the dance floor much further down the line to add even more gaming glitz and glamor. Appearing as part of the Battle Pass for those with dedication to the cause, there were two hairstyle options and five variants, all with subtle added elements to crank up the diva details on the disco-obsessed Outfit. Reverse Disco is the variant that really stands out from the dancing crowd, with a glimmering silver look that makes others stop and stare while she struts and poses.

**SPARKLE
SCYTHE**

**SPARKLE
STRIDER**

FACT

For the Season X Battle Pass, there was some cool remixing of existing famous Outfits... streamers and players loved it!

FUR FORCE
TAKING CREATURE COMFORTS TO THE EXTREME

FENNIX

INTRODUCED IN: SEASON X
RARITY: RARE

Trying to outfox this Outfit could take several seasons! Fennix is a giant fox with a cunning knack of combining animalistic power with human-like craft and guile. His eyes, though, look almost alien and the shoulder and kneepads prove he's ready to go to ground and dig in deep to register a victory. Fennix enters the Item Shop every now and then but, as foxes are nocturnal, you may need to stay up all night just to catch a glimpse of him...

FOXPACK

GETAWAY GANG
WHEN A DEAL IS GOING DOWN, DON'T DRESS LIKE A JOKER

DARK WILD CARD

INTRODUCED IN: SEASON X
SERIES: DARK

Outfits are unlocked through purchasing in the Item Shop or as part of the Battle Pass, but when they become available by another way, it makes them very special. Dark Wild Card was part of the Dark Reflections Pack, which also had the Dark Jonesy and Dark Red Knight Outfits, plus three cool cosmetics. With a sleek purple suit, black waistcoat, and smart tie, Dark Wild Card is always ready to deal out some shade.

FACT

Dark Wild Card is a re-skin of the popular Wild Card Outfit from Season 5. Dark was a new series first introduced with Dark Bomber in Season 6.

CUFF CASE

HEIST

INTRODUCED IN: SEASON 9
RARITY: RARE

With a similar style to Dark Wild Card, at least in the top half, Heist looks capable of pulling off a smash-and-grab job around the island with very little bother. The jacket and shirt combo is contradicted, though, by his white shorts and red shoes, and where have his socks disappeared to? There are so many questions to ask this conspicuous chap.

GOLDEN TOUCH
ALL THAT GLITTERS IS... GOLD

GOLD DAGGER PACK

MIDAS

INTRODUCED IN: CHAPTER 2: SEASON 2
RARITY: LEGENDARY

Reaching Tier 100 was a top priority for all Battle
Pass holders this season for one simple reason—
unlocking this bejeweled character! Looking like
a dapper businessman-zombie cross, Midas has
the golden touch, quite literally, as he can turn
weapons and vehicles pure gold for a match. His
Ghost and Shadow variants are stunningly striking
as well, and the Gold Dagger Pack Back Bling, Golden
King Harvesting Tool, and Midas Memory Wrap
boost the dazzling effect of this secret agent.

GOLDEN KING

FACT

Midas gets his name from the
famous King Midas, of ancient
Greek mythology, who was
claimed to have the ability to turn
everything he touched into gold.

GREEN CLOVER
SAINT PATRICK WOULD BE PROUD

LUCKY RIDER

INTRODUCED IN: SEASON 8
RARITY: EPIC

The Green Clover set draws heavily on the luck of the Irish theme, so pick up Lucky Rider from the Item Shop and chances are you'll score a brilliant— and perhaps rather fluky—result while in this Outfit. Dressed as the coolest motorcycle rider you'll ever see, select the Emerald Smasher Harvesting Tool and Rainbow Clover Back Bling for a display that says you're going Irish all the way.

EMERALD SMASHER

FACT

With the Season 8 Battle Pass, you could earn the Clovers Contrail, to ideally give you an extra boost of luck as you made your way from the Battle Bus.

GRUMBLE GANG
BE A GOOD BOY

CHEW TOY

CHOW DOWN

DOGGO

INTRODUCED IN: SEASON 9
RARITY: EPIC

Pugs are super-cute and everyone's favorite dog, right? Yet it wasn't until Season 9 that these incredible animals were given their own Outfit in the Item Shop. However, it was totally worth the wait because Doggo's deadpan expression, striped hoodie, and skinny jeans shout a design that's like nothing else in Fortnite. With two further selectable styles providing a festive Santa and military hooded Doggo, this creature is both cute and pet-rifying.

DOGGIE BAG

FACT

Keep a watchful eye on Doggo's face when it busts out emotes—the range of expressions will crack you up!

CATASTROPHE

INTRODUCED IN: SEASON X
RARITY: RARE

The cute cat ears and reversed baseball cap look was "purr-fected" by the default Lynx Outfit in Season 7. Feline fans were delighted to see Catastrophe enter the Item Shop a few seasons later, with a gentle nod to the animal through her headgear but also an energetic soldier presence in tough boots mixed with biohazard protective gear. Bundled with the Outfit is the chunky Toxic Kitty Back Bling, complete with a kitty-shaped hazard mask that shows Catastrophe is not afraid to tackle dangerous situations.

JAGGED EDGE

HEAVY HITTER
LANDING BLOW AFTER BLOW

SLEDGE

INTRODUCED IN: SEASON X
RARITY: RARE

Terrorize the landscape with this costume that's ready for the battlefield. This warrior carries a quality that commands instant respect, with Sledge looking as though he could skydive from the clouds and ambush a building without even getting out of first gear. His suit is solid, sharp, and adaptable under any scenario and the Stronghold Back Bling and Impact Edge Harvesting Tool serves up a bundle that delivers a knockout blow. Heavy Hitter is a set packed with power.

IMPACT EDGE

HOPPITY HEIST
BEATING YOU TO THE PRIZE

BOLD BAR

HOPPER

INTRODUCED IN: SEASON 8
RARITY: RARE

Springtime is a fun time, full of chocolate, bunnies, and candy. Hopper merges all three of these, with a selectable Egghead style showing a tasty Easter egg with a tiny top hat perched on it. The default version is already based on a decorated egg theme, which is matched by a white pattern across the pink jacket and dotted green shoes. Opt for the Bunny Bag Back Bling and Bold Bar Harvesting Tool, which looks like a metal candy cane, and you're ready to break up any Springtime event.

HOT AIR
LIFE IS BUT A BREEZE

BENDIE

INTRODUCED IN: SEASON 8
RARITY: RARE

Equip the Bendie Inflator Back Bling and create an air of excitement and intrigue by breezing through the battlefield as Bendie. He appears harmless enough, filled with gas and blowing merrily in the wind, but this happy dude can still outgun an opponent when the opportunity arises.

FLIMSIE FLAIL

BENDIE INFLATOR

TWISTIE

INTRODUCED IN: SEASON 8
RARITY: RARE

Bendie's partner in crime, Twistie, is not averse to throwing uncontrollable shapes and also possesses an unnaturally positive outlook. The Twistie Inflator Back Bling cranks up the air pressure and in duos, this party-loving pair form a partnership that looks like a pushover but in reality is tough to outdo.

TWISTIE INFLATOR

ICE KINGDOM
COLD AND CALCULATED

SHIVER

INTRODUCED IN: CHAPTER 2: SEASON 1
RARITY: EPIC

Remember that feeling you get when you walk into a freezing room and the hairs on the back of your neck stand up? That's what happens every time Shiver is on the scene and she makes no excuses for eliminating players in a cold and calculated manner. There's a devilish streak to this Outfit too, and you don't want to be on the receiving end of that terrifying tail.

ICEBRINGER

FACT

Shiver is the first non-royal Outfit from the Ice Kingdom set, with The Ice King and The Ice Queen making a frosty appearance in Season 7.

IMMORTAL SANDS
TIMELESS WARRIORS NEVER CLOCK OFF

SANDSTORM

INTRODUCED IN: SEASON 9
RARITY: RARE

Rare Outfits cost a little less V-Bucks than Epic and Legendary, so when Sandstorm blew into the Item Shop in the blue Rare category, it was a bargain not to be missed. Plus, this fearsome female has three selectable styles, with the covered face style giving Sandstorm a mysterious edge. Gold decals glisten throughout, from the hood trim to the shoelaces, and lend an expensive edge to this Outfit.

SCIMITAR

INTRODUCED IN: SEASON 9
RARITY: RARE

As Sandstorm's male ally, Scimitar is enrobed in a darker dress with three-quarter-length baggy pants and a stylish jacket with extravagant gold piping. He, too, can be selected with and without his mask and whether he's covered up or revealing his chiseled features, Scimitar doesn't look the type to ever leave you deserted in the sand dunes. "Deserted," get it? Oh well...

FACT

Chrono is a Contrail that is part of the Immortal Sands set. Equip it to watch a sparkling golden glow emit from Sandstorm and Scimitar as they descend!

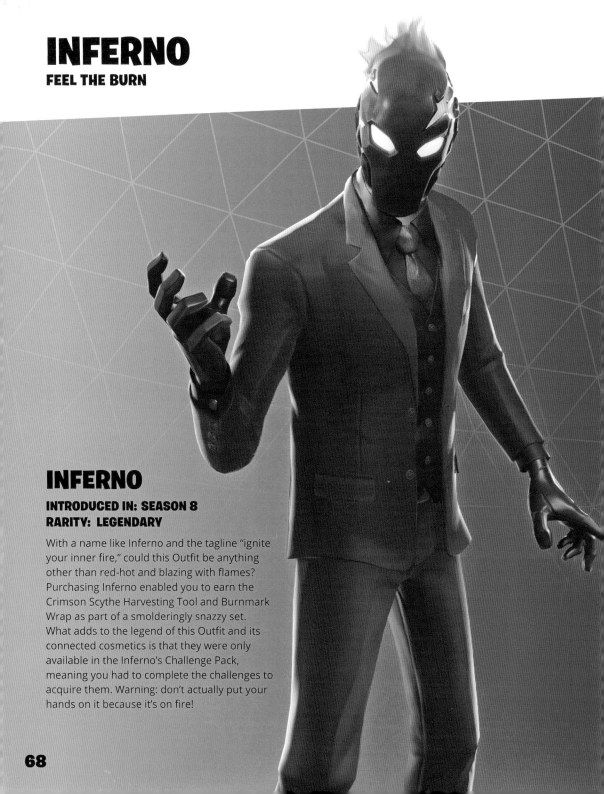

INFERNO
FEEL THE BURN

INFERNO

INTRODUCED IN: SEASON 8
RARITY: LEGENDARY

With a name like Inferno and the tagline "ignite your inner fire," could this Outfit be anything other than red-hot and blazing with flames? Purchasing Inferno enabled you to earn the Crimson Scythe Harvesting Tool and Burnmark Wrap as part of a smolderingly snazzy set. What adds to the legend of this Outfit and its connected cosmetics is that they were only available in the Inferno's Challenge Pack, meaning you had to complete the challenges to acquire them. Warning: don't actually put your hands on it because it's on fire!

INTERSTELLAR
REACH FOR THE STARS

LUMINOS

INTRODUCED IN: SEASON 8
RARITY: EPIC

Blending purple, turquoise, silver, and black, Luminos lights up his surroundings and clearly isn't the most camouflaged of Outfits. But standing out from the crowd shows you're not scared of a challenge and such a spectrum will mark this dude out as a colorful character in more ways than one. With owl-like eyes, Luminos is also a wise head on vibrant shoulders.

ASTRAL AXE

FACT
Luminos hit the Item Shop at the same time as Dream, which is another mystical, purple-glowing Outfit.

KATA TECH
MEAN MACHINES MEAN BUSINESS

COPPER WASP

INTRODUCED IN: SEASON 9
RARITY: EPIC

As a super-strength android with martial arts in his locker, Copper Wasp buzzes into action when the threat level rises. Underneath his blue-gray gi suit, which has been ripped and frayed at the shoulders and ankles to accommodate powerful limbs, is a copper bronzed body that's primed for a rapid response. Will Copper Wasp choose fight or flight? You know the answer...

POWER PUNCH

TSUKI

INTRODUCED IN: SEASON 9
RARITY: RARE

With a strong feeling of Japanese manga about her, Tsuki is an unpredictable and unforgiving android designed as the perfect partner to Copper Wasp. She rocks a mostly off-white gray tone, broken defiantly by penetrating red eyes, and when Tsuki's matched with the Tahna Back Bling from the Kata Tech set, the atmosphere around her is as chilling as her stare.

KEY FORCE

UNLOCKING POTENTIAL IS THE KEY

MASTER KEY

INTRODUCED IN: SEASON 8
RARITY: EPIC

Straight up this is an Outfit for ultra-cool cats, but throw in the selectable and unlockable styles and Master Key is a range of looks to purr over. It was first available for Battle Pass players, with the unmasked variant unlocked at Tier 87. Reaching Tier 99 saw the masked Outfit unleashed, which sports a golden tiger face covering that neatly matches the gloves, decals on the jacket, and of course the golden keys on the chest and hip. Completing the Overtime Challenges saw the White Style Master Key unlocked and its simplified color scheme of black, silver, and green looks stunning.

MASTER PORTAL

LOCKPICK

73

MOLTEN BATTLE HOUND

INTRODUCED IN: SEASON 8
SERIES: LAVA

Season 8 saw a volcano erupt and lava spew across the island, so the arrival of the Lava Series was very timely. Part of the special Lava Legends Pack only, which means the Outfit wasn't in the Item Shop, Molten Battle Hound is a fire-breathing dog-human with red-hot juices pumping through it. Along with the Molten Crested Cape Back Bling and Lavawing Glider, this getup follows a scorched-earth policy!

MOLTEN CRESTED CAPE

LAVAWING

MOLTEN VALKYRIE

INTRODUCED IN: SEASON 8
SERIES: LAVA

Keep the fire burning with this blistering Outfit. Complementing her male counterpart, Molten Valkyrie is also laced with lava and it's safe to assume that everything she touches will go up in smoke. The Molten Valkyrie Wings Back Bling finishes an appearance that keeps temperatures rising.

FACT

Just as the Lava Legends Pack arrived to turn up the heat, the Floor is Lava Limited Time Mode also appeared. Season 8 was on fire, people!

MECHANIMAL

BEASTMODE

INTRODUCED IN: SEASON 8
RARITY: EPIC

Time to meet the coolest mechanical-looking animal person ever! Beastmode is a frightening name and the heavy metal armor and headgear is a sign of strength, but you can't help but giggle a little at the cute hand-painted teeth and eyes. This Outfit has some great selectable styles, with Rhino, Jackal, Jaguar, and Lion filling out the fearsome foursome. Strap on each style's V6 Back Bling and let the animal kingdom conquer all.

FUEL (LION)

V6

RHINO

JACKEL

LION

JAGUAR

MAULER
(JACKAL)

77

METRO SQUAD
THE ART OF BEING STREET SMART

SHOT CALLER

INTRODUCED IN: SEASON X
RARITY: RARE

Calling the shots is what every player should be aiming for in Battle Royale. The comfy, street-style pants and sweater set up a relaxed look, with the scarf and cap still keeping this guy's identity a little under wraps. The Utility Pack Back Bling makes sure Shot Caller is prepared for all eventualities, because he always wants to stay in control.

METRO MACHETES

FACT
Shot Caller is a Rare Outfit in more ways than one—it was only in the Item Shop for two days after its first release!

MIDNIGHT STAR
WHEN THE CLOCK STRIKES TWELVE...

HAZE

INTRODUCED IN:
CHAPTER 2: SEASON 1
RARITY: RARE

Simple, clean Outfits with a two-tone color scheme can rack up plenty of plaudits. Rocking black pants and a black crop top with just a pink star emblem to match her locks, this lady's understated fashion has an overpowering impact. Choose the Outfit from the Item Shop and you'll be tempted to run the Extreme selectable style and cast yourself as a vampire-styled warrior complete with red demonic horns. Haze could really cloud the judgment of your opponents.

STARSHOT

THE BRAT

INTRODUCED IN: CHAPTER 2: SEASON 1
RARITY: RARE

There is just something so fun, fantastical, and freakish about running and leaping around the island dressed as your favorite food. The Brat is a fave with many players, sporting a mustard-flavored sausage and bun under rock-star shades and cap. The selectable style No Hat reveals a rounded top end that looks totally tasty—just make sure you don't get too distracted and eat into your gaming time.

FACT

The Loose Links Contrail is included with the Outfit, letting you fall from the Battle Bus with sausages flailing and waving around you!

MOONBONE
SUNDOWN MEANS A SHOWDOWN

NIGHTWITCH

INTRODUCED IN: SEASON 8
RARITY: EPIC

Scary things can happen at night, and you don't want to be met with this dusky destroyer under the cover of darkness. She is a daunting warrior decked in tribal-style clothing and although there are pockets of color and details, the impression Nightwitch gives is one of gloomy terror and trouble. Be brave and choose this Outfit from the Item Shop, though, because it will strike fear into your opponents.

CUDDLE DOLL

FACT
The Cuddle Doll Back Bling is a mini version of the Cuddle Team Leader Outfit from Season 2, just with added spookiness!

SHAMAN

INTRODUCED IN: SEASON 8
RARITY: EPIC

Matching Nightwitch with a traditional carved facemask, braided locks, and epic elements of battle from years gone by, this Outfit also goes heavy on the bone factor. Sharp fragments are featured around the gloves, shoulders, and waist, giving Shaman a cutting edge to be wary of.

NEOCHASER
HUNT OR BE HUNTED

ETHER

INTRODUCED IN: SEASON 9
RARITY: EPIC

Practicality need not compromise style, and Ether is fit for claiming a Victory Royale while still looking slick and polished. Check out the long colorful protective overcoat with a funky transparent collar fixed just under the gas mask. Modern and menacing, hanging out with Ether is a real gas!

WEB WRECKER

CNXN

VERSA

INTRODUCED IN: SEASON 9
RARITY: EPIC

Try not to be fooled by the thick visor, because Versa has eyes on everything and won't hesitate to rain down her skills on unsuspecting enemies. The standout element from her Outfit is the awesome jacket that has a see-through barrier that looks like it could repel any force. A close inspection could lead to elimination, though.

NEON JUNGLE
IT'S A BLAZING MAZE OF COLOR OUT THERE

HEART GRID

BUNNYWOLF

INTRODUCED IN: CHAPTER 2: SEASON 2
RARITY: EPIC

Pure animal power, and plenty of glowing bright colors, are what give Bunnywolf her distinct style. Appearing as a mix of futuristic pet and aerobics dancer, this fan fave has three selectable styles of Wolf, Neon Bunny, and default Bunny. The psychedelic silliness doesn't stop there, though, as the reactive Outfit can be changed while you have your Harvesting Tool or Weapon out. Pretty cool, hey? Be quick to pick up this prized bunny whenever it cycles into the Item Shop.

DIAMOND GRID

LLION

INTRODUCED IN: CHAPTER 2: SEASON 2
RARITY: EPIC

Prowling the neon night is an easy mission with this Outfit. Decked with sparkling shades and lines, particularly on the arms and neck, LLion also has selectable Neon Llama and Neon Tiger styles for a range of awesome animal effects. Just like his female counterpart Bunnywolf, he has a special trick of switching styles when you cycle between your Harvesting Tool and Weapon.

NITEHARE
DARE TO DREAM

NITEHARE

INTRODUCED IN: SEASON 8
RARITY: EPIC

The Easter element of Season 8 saw this weird-looking bunny bounce into action. Not your typical perky pet, it's very somber with sad eyes and drooping ears that definitely portray an animal that doesn't enjoy being cuddled and pampered. Nitehare's Floppy Back Bling is wrapped in chains, just like Nitehare, to dampen the spirit of anyone that catches a glimpse.

FLOPPY

STEEL CARROT

OPEN WATER
SINK OR SWIM

DEPTH DEALER

INTRODUCED IN: CHAPTER 2: SEASON 1
RARITY: RARE

Chapter 2: Season 1 opened the floodgates on the island and saw water features, swimming, fishing, and boat riding. The Open Water set suited this theme perfectly and Depth Dealer's getup of an all-action waterproof top, with marine-colored camouflaged pants and a matching facing mask, make him an ideal candidate for any missions involving the wet stuff.

TACKLE BOX

SKY TRAWLER

ANGLER
AXES

OUTCAST

INTRODUCED IN: CHAPTER 2: SEASON 1
RARITY: RARE

There is something fishy going on here, but don't fret—Outcast is packed with floats and gear and just loves to reel in a big catch. The selectable A.L.T.E.R. and E.G.O. variants switch Outcast from yellow to gray with a turquoise beanie, and the Fresh Catch Back Bling is strapped with two giant fishing hooks. She'll wait as long as necessary for the bait to be taken!

WAVEBREAKER

INTRODUCED IN: CHAPTER 2: SEASON 1
RARITY: RARE

Wading in for the Wavebreaker Pack rewarded players with a great-value bundle of the Wavebreaker Outfit, Dry Bag Back Bling, Swell Striker Harvesting Tool and 600 V-Bucks. The Outfit is similar to Depth Dealer and when she brandishes the oversized Swell Striker, she has an appearance that has others waving goodbye in a battle.

TURK VS RIPTIDE

INTRODUCED IN:
CHAPTER 2: SEASON 1
RARITY: RARE

Getting involved with the Battle Pass was the only way to capture this iconic A.L.T.E.R. and E.G.O. Outfit after the frenzy it created at the beginning of Chapter 2: Season 1. Turk, the heroic-looking fisherman, was unleashed easily enough but Riptide required a little more mission-based achievement before he appeared. Riptide is much older than Turk and has the experience to hook prey with no drama.

PIZZA PIT

CHEESY COSTUMES FOR TOPPING THE LEADERBOARD

AXERONI

PJ PEPPERONI

INTRODUCED IN: SEASON X
RARITY: RARE

Tomatohead and Nightshade, from Season 3 and Season 6 respectively, made Pizza Pit an extremely sought-after set. PJ Pepperoni continues the fast food theme and her relaxed, super-comfortable green and orange costume is splattered with cheese, pizza, and slicing wheel motifs... even Tomatohead himself appears on her Outfit!

EXTRA CHEESE

FACT

PJ Pepperoni uses the same all-in-one, hooded lounge-style suit as Onesie, a Season 7 Battle Pass Outfit that's part of the cool Durrr Burger set.

POLAR ACE
THIS IS SNOW JOKE

ARCTICA

INTRODUCED IN: CHAPTER 2: SEASON 1
RARITY: RARE

When snow and ice are on the way, Arctica won't have a problem with the freezing conditions. She is cozy and warm inside her shiny, padded jumpsuit and those pink reflective shades mirror the tinge in her shoulder-length hair. The Modern Summit Back Bling contains ropes and climbing tools to keep her on top of the opposition.

SNOW PATROLLER

INTRODUCED IN: CHAPTER 2: SEASON 1
RARITY: RARE

At first glance, he looks just like the sort of strong hero and safe pair of hands you would crave for if you became stuck in a snowdrift. But look again and you'll notice the teeth tracks on his mask and the skeleton-like prints on his black gloves. Does this mean Snow Patroller has a dark side?

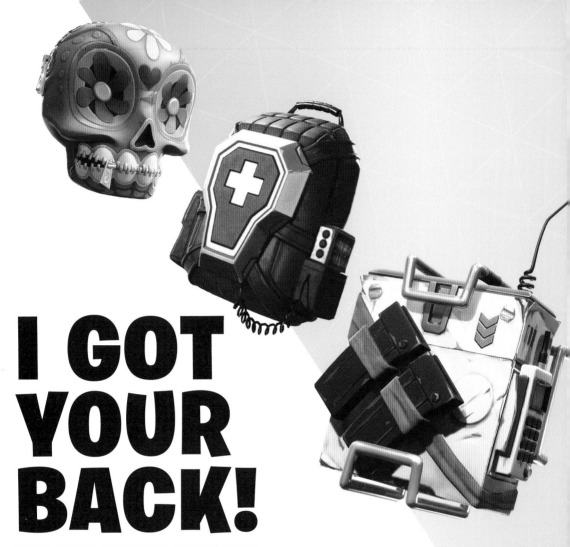

I GOT YOUR BACK!

LOOK THROUGH SOME OF THE MOST EYE-CATCHING BACK BLINGS OF ALL TIME

What's your favorite thing about customizing and collecting in Fortnite? Perhaps it's picking up a fresh selection of Outfits, including those with selectable styles? Maybe impressive Gliders, Harvesting Tools, or Wraps top your list of likes? For many players, though, strapping on breathtaking Back Bling ranks highly among the things they like to spend time doing in the game. You see it all the time, so you might as well choose the most striking and spectacular from the Item Shop and Battle Passes! Here's an epic selection of some popular Back Blings...

QUACK PACK

INTRODUCED IN: SEASON 9
RARITY: UNCOMMON

Everyone... duck! Quack Pack was part of the 14 Days of Summer event and players went full steam to collect this cute bath-time buddy.

BALL BLING

INTRODUCED IN:
CHAPTER 2: SEASON 2
RARITY: EPIC

Bundled with the 8-Ball Vs Scratch Outfit and with selectable styles, this Back Bling is a pool player's dream. Rack 'em up!

LIGHTNING CLOAK

INTRODUCED IN: SEASON 9
RARITY: LEGENDARY

Legendary Back Bling costs a little more, but you can see where the extra V-Bucks go— Lightning Cloak is mysterious with epic superhero vibes.

PINEAPPLE STRUMMER

INTRODUCED IN: SEASON 8
RARITY: RARE

Make some sweet music around the map. Pineapple Strummer is a cosmetic to get you licking your lips.

COOLER

INTRODUCED IN: SEASON 9
RARITY: RARE

It's a good idea to pack snacks for your adventure, but why does it look like Fishstick's hand is sticking out? Totally maxing out the weird factor!

BANANA BRIEFCASE

INTRODUCED IN:
CHAPTER 2: SEASON 2
RARITY: EPIC

Need extra energy for a Battle Royale? Equip this Back Bling for a fruity supply that could make the opposition go bananas!

SPECTRAL SPINE

INTRODUCED IN: SEASON 9
RARITY: RARE

Entering the Item Shop on the first day of Season 9, it made a big opening impression alongside the Cryptic Outfit.

PERFECT WINGS

INTRODUCED IN: SEASON 9
SERIES: SHADOW

The Shadows Rising Pack has three Back Blings, including this set of wings that makes your character look absolutely heavenly.

RAINBOW CLOVER

INTRODUCED IN: SEASON 8
RARITY: EPIC

The Lucky Rider Outfit totally bosses it with this themed Back Bling from the Green Clover set, but the cosmetic looks classy with loads of other Outfits too.

SLICE 'N DICE

INTRODUCED IN: SEASON 8
RARITY: EPIC

Some Back Bling make you, and your enemies, giggle...but Slice 'n Dice strikes pure fear. There's no joking with this strapped on your back.

JET SET

INTRODUCED IN: SEASON 9
RARITY: EPIC

Pink doesn't match every Outfit, but it goes perfectly with Mecha Team Leader. Time to power up.

SMOOTHIE

INTRODUCED IN: SEASON 9
RARITY: RARE

Introduced as your "blended banana buddy," give yourself a smooth and healthy style with a crazy Back Bling from the Bunker Days set.

HAYSTACKS

INTRODUCED IN: SEASON 8
RARITY: UNCOMMON

If all else fails, just try camping out in a crop field and blending in with the background.

TAKEOUT

INTRODUCED IN: SEASON X
RARITY: EPIC

With extra ketchup and mustard at the ready, this saucy Back Bling is one for the hungry players. Napkins not included.

GWINNY

INTRODUCED IN:
CHAPTER 2: SEASON 1
RARITY: EPIC

As if a lovable penguin isn't delightful enough, it's wrapped in a pink and red fluffy scarf. Such a pretty pack for your back.

ZOMBALL

INTRODUCED IN:
CHAPTER 2: SEASON 1
RARITY: RARE

Is mixing zombies and soccer a smart move? Probably not, given how menacing this cosmetic has turned out. What even IS that gooey green stuff?

DORSAL DESTROYER

INTRODUCED IN:
CHAPTER 2: SEASON 2
RARITY: RARE

It's a small fishy creature, packed in a deep-sea diving suit with mini weapons. What's unusual about that?

SHARK'S TANK

INTRODUCED IN:
CHAPTER 2: SEASON 1
RARITY: RARE

Don't go creeping up on a player sporting this predatory Back Bling—chances are they're gonna bite back.

POLAR LEGENDS
PUT THE COMPETITION ON ICE

CODENAME E.L.F. (MINT)

INTRODUCED IN: CHAPTER 2: SEASON 1
RARITY: RARE

Originally released around Christmas back in Season 2, Codename E.L.F. returned with a cool additional style as part of the Polar Legends Pack. Referred to as Minty, this style of Codename E.L.F. possesses glowing green eyes, bright colors on the gloves, kneepads, and jacket trim and an overall moodier demeanor thanks to the purple shades. Minty is fresh but formidable, which is quite a combination to pull off!

FROZEN FISHSTICK

INTRODUCED IN: CHAPTER 2: SEASON 1
SERIES: FROZEN

As re-skins go, this caused quite a stir as Fortnite players adore the original Season 7 Fishstick's Outfit, but luckily they also lapped up this chilling character. Looking a little frazzled by the frozen water, it's an Outfit that brings players a warm feeling inside every time he drops on the island.

FROZEN NOG OPS

INTRODUCED IN: SEASON 2: CHAPTER 1
SERIES: FROZEN

The Polar Legends Pack was bursting with cosmetics—the four Outfits on these pages plus two Back Blings—for a festive Fortnite treat. Frozen Nog Ops takes the original Nog Ops Outfit, from Christmas 2017, and turns the red, green, and white Santa colors into a scheme of icy blue. Even her frosty lips make her look like she's been outside in the cold for days!

CASTLE PEAKS

THE DEVOURER

INTRODUCED IN: SEASON 2: CHAPTER 1
SERIES: FROZEN

Coming bundled with its own flashy Emote and two selectable styles that are with and without frost, The Devourer is a monstrous Outfit in more ways than one. Seasoned players were already aware of its existence before Chapter 2: Season 1, though, as a giant-sized rendition was part of the Polar Peak event in Season 8.

SKYE

INTRODUCED IN:
CHAPTER 2: SEASON 2
RARITY: EPIC

The least "secret agent"-looking of the secret agent Outfits from the Battle Pass and unlocked at Tier 80, Skye still has plenty of tricks up her sleeve. Or rather, "under her hat"... Skye's Ghost and Shadow unlockable variants are different to the likes of Meowscles and Brutus, in that she has a more subtle color change and not the usual dark or pale selection. She also takes on the cool gold enlightened Outfit once Tier 300 is reached.

OLLIE

FACT

Skye's Ollie Glider actually appears from her hat and is a cute fluffy creature with teardrop-shaped wings.

ADVENTURE PACK

RACER ROYALE
FROM PODIUM POSITION TO PODIUM PLACINGS

SLINGSHOT

INTRODUCED IN: SEASON X
RARITY: UNCOMMON

Players raced over to the Item Shop when Slingshot sped into sight as the third Outfit in the Racer Royale set. Just like Whiplash, her racing buddy, she sports a track-ready driving suit with checkered accents and racing gloves to prove she'll jump behind the wheel and take the finishing flag in style. Swoop in with the Checker Glider for the ultimate way to announce your high-speed appearance.

CHECKER

RAGING STORM
FIGHTING NATURE IS A LOSING BATTLE

STORM EYE

TEMPEST

INTRODUCED IN: SEASON 9
RARITY: LEGENDARY

The Tempest Outfit is a spectacular combat suit and there appears to be a storm raging beneath his skin—check out the flashing electro shocks and pulses rippling around his torso and arms. Under the helmet is a pair of eyes that flicker a pinky-purple beam. Keep watch on the Item Shop if you're tempted to try out Tempest.

LIGHTNING CLOAK

FACT

Tempest's Lightning Cloak Back Bling is torn and shredded around the edges—he's clearly a guy that doesn't hide in a storm.

STORM BOLT

GRIM FABLE

INTRODUCED IN: CHAPTER 2: SEASON 1
RARITY: EPIC

In Season 6, Red Riding's Fable sprung a surprise storyline or two as a sweet-looking character not afraid to take on the bad guys (or bad wolves). Grim Fable is not a straightforward re-skin though, coming with her own fearsome fashion and a selectable hooded style showing off a wolf and prickly teeth. Her mission is to write her own story and no one, furry or otherwise, will get in her way.

BIG BAD AXE

PACK LEADER

ROUGHNECK

GETTING BUSINESS DONE BEFORE THE CLOSE OF PLAY

BIZ

INTRODUCED IN: SEASON 9
RARITY: RARE

Sure, there's a lot going on here, but the essence of this Outfit is that of a mysterious streetwise competitor out to cause a stir. The black and white socks and dress clash with the bronze and blue jacket and shades, but you get the feeling Biz is not the kind of lady who wants to blend into the background. With her left arm beefed up with padding and canisters, she looks ready to take on all comers.

ROYALE HEARTS
ALL'S FAIR IN LOVE AND WAR

CUDDLE CRUISER

BUNDLES

INTRODUCED IN: CHAPTER 2: SEASON 1
RARITY: RARE

As one of the most extensive, well-known, and long-lasting sets, gamers just gotta love Outfits from Royale Hearts, yeah? This big, off-white winter teddy bear wears a scarf to keep warm, which is pink and red in homage to the Legendary Cuddle Team Leader from Season 2. Take a peek at the scratches on the cheeks, too, as a mark that this creature is prepared to defend her territory.

CUDDLE PAW

FACT

Bundles is a reactive Outfit—watch it react in its perpetual cold temperature, as strange signals appear around those cute ears!

BROKEN HEART

SNUGGS

INTRODUCED IN: CHAPTER 2: SEASON 1
RARITY: RARE

It's pretty clear from Snuggs's ratty fur, missing eye and sewn-up mouth that this is one teddy bear in need of plenty of TLC. The black color scheme looks utterly immense on the island, especially when contrasted with the hot pink details. If you go down in the woods today, you too might be in for a big surprise....

CUPID'S DAGGER

STONEHEART

INTRODUCED IN: SEASON X
RARITY: EPIC

Ever since he appeared in Season 2, Love Ranger has been a lonely lad. Now, finally, he has a female friend after Stoneheart came and lit up his world. The statuesque love warrior looks super-slick with the Wings of Love Back Bling, which is another match for Love Ranger's Love Wings. This pair knows how to capture hearts (and opponents) in perfect harmony.

WINGS OF LOVE

RPM
FORTNITE'S FASTEST THRILL-SEEKERS

HARD CHARGER

INTRODUCED IN: SEASON X
RARITY: UNCOMMON

Guys and girls in the RPM set are just not happy with revealing their full identity, as both Burnout and Redline from Season 3 and 5 also hid behind a helmet. That pair are motorcyclists, whereas Hard Charger is more a freefalling man of the skies, even though there's not a parachute in sight. He'll just have to make do with the cool Stunt Cycle Glider to make his memorable entrance.

CHAINED CLEAVER

PAYBACK

INTRODUCED IN: SEASON X
RARITY: RARE

Payback does show us some of her facial features; however, she is still quite a cryptic character with her upturned jacket collar helping to keep her integrity intact. Her spiky traits are obvious (have you seen those pads on her shoulders, knees, and hands?) and you'd be advised not to push her to her limits unless you want to see some serious, erm, payback!

RUINATION
RULING FROM THE WRECKAGE

DREAD

RUIN

INTRODUCED IN: SEASON 8
RARITY: LEGENDARY

Step forward Ruin—an Outfit that can frighten the enemy AND the player using it in equal measure! Unlocked through hard work by completing the Discovery Challenges in the Battle Pass, it is as dark and disturbing as Outfits can come and the glowing red openings around Ruin's body back up his utterly imposing aura. If it's all too much to look at, try operating this monster with your eyes closed—after all, that's what those he comes up against will be doing.

DYING LIGHT

SCALLYWAGS
BRINGING THE GAME INTO DISREPUTE

BLACKHEART

INTRODUCED IN: SEASON 8
RARITY: LEGENDARY

Blackheart remains a truly standout Outfit in the Fortnite universe. A Tier 1 reward in the Battle Pass, a further seven variants were unlocked through progress in the Blackheart Challenges. Scallywags is a nautical-themed set and the pirate power of Blackheart becomes apparent as one of his hands changes to a hook and a wooden peg replaces his lower leg. Remain in shipshape condition to get the better of this wily warrior.

FACT
As well as Blackheart's eight selectable styles, he also has four clothing color variants.

HIGH SEAS

109

BOOTY BUOY

BUCCANEER

INTRODUCED IN: SEASON 8
RARITY: RARE

Keep the pirate party going with this salty sea-faring raider. Thanks to a choice of two selectable styles, swapping in a variant with an eye patch and jaunty upturned hat could fool the opposition into thinking Buccaneer is a jovial figure just here for a laugh. How wrong they would be.

SWAG SMASHER

DARING DUELIST

INTRODUCED IN: SEASON 8
RARITY: EPIC

Considering herself a cut above her low-level shipmates, this crusader never shirks combat duties and is most happy when squaring up for a one-on-one duel in a daring raid. The Slice 'N Dice Back Bling straps perfectly to her and any attempts to launch a cheeky foray against her will be dealt with swiftly. Heed the warning.

SEA WOLF

INTRODUCED IN: SEASON 8
RARITY: RARE

Harking back to an age when the brave and the bold set sail for glory, Sea Wolf has both of those characteristics in bucket loads. Toggle between the selectable styles to choose either a fancy hat with feather and waistcoat or a red bandana with a smart goatee beard. Sea Wolf is a pack leader in every sense.

111

SCARLET DRAGON
RED SIGNALS DANGER

DEMI

INTRODUCED IN: SEASON 9
RARITY: EPIC

The cool cyborg arm reminded many fans of
Shadow Ops from Season 2, but unlike that
Stealth Syndicate Outfit, Demi became available
through the Battle Pass. Reaching Tier 87 unlocked
this powerful but clean-looking character, with
the interest ramped up even further with the
selectable Night variant from the Overtime
Challenges. Dashing around in search of a Victory
Royale while wearing high heels is not usually
recommended, but Demi rarely puts a foot wrong.

**SCARLET
SCYTHE**

SHOOTING STARS
METEOR YOU ON THE OTHER SIDE

ASTRA

INTRODUCED IN: CHAPTER 2: SEASON 1
RARITY: EPIC

Released into the Item Shop on the very last day of 2019, Astra saw the New Year in with bling and style. If stars, constellations, and sky-high drama are your thing—or if you just want a lustrous night-themed Outfit—select it and then choose either the star or default option. The star variant looks a bit like pajamas, which is cool, and default serves up more tiny sparkles and glitzy lines. The sky's the limit with this Outfit!

FACT
You can furnish this Outfit with the set's Shining Star Back Bling, which blends in brilliantly with Astra's look, to be a true leading light in Fortnite.

SHORT FUSE
GOING OUT WITH A BANG

BOMBS AWAY!

WILD BLAST

TNTINA

INTRODUCED IN: CHAPTER 2: SEASON 2
RARITY: EPIC

Do you get hyped about explosive action? Then TNTina is the Outfit for you, as she is bursting with style and tricks. Not only does this Battle Pass character have the unlockable Ghost and Shadow styles that became popular in Chapter 2: Season 2, but it also boasts the enlightened golden style once Tier 220 is accomplished. The most satisfying part of TNTina, though, is her exclusive Boom emote—drop this into your play to stun and shock those around you. Riding in while standing on top of the Bombs Away! Glider is also a look that's unlike anything else.

SIEGE STRIKE
INNER STRENGTH EQUALS WINNING STRENGTH

DEADFALL

INTRODUCED IN: SEASON X
RARITY: UNCOMMON

Check out the team colors on show here. The Siege Strike set is made up of four identical Outfits, all using a different warrior character, and is perfect for a squad to coordinate with and take down enemies. Urban and modern camo styles are always immense on the eye and effective in a Battle Royale.

KNOCKOUT

INTRODUCED IN: SEASON X
RARITY: UNCOMMON

Knockout stands out from his set teammates with his short, cropped hair, but he matches them with a muscular physique and cool camouflage across the shirt and pants. It has to be said, though, that the masks do little to protect these folks' identity—it's there for effect rather than necessity.

SNAKEPIT

INTRODUCED IN: SEASON X
RARITY: UNCOMMON

The wavy blond locks are a familiar style to players and in this instance they tie in well with the golden-gray stripes of the Siege Strike branding. Snakepit is not the most welcoming of Outfit names, and just as well because he's the sort of soldier with a sting in his tail and fully fixated on striking out at whoever gets in his way.

VICE

INTRODUCED IN: SEASON X
RARITY: UNCOMMON

Completing the set is Vice, who closely resembles Deadfall in the hairstyle stakes, but has a more carefree bouffant approach to his appearance up top. He carries the classic new-age military demeanor perfectly and the shoulder tattoo complements his urban warrior look.

117

SINGULARITY

GOING SOLO

SINGULARITY

INTRODUCED IN: SEASON 9
RARITY: LEGENDARY

In the Season 8 Battle Pass, the magic number was 90. That was the total of Fortbytes needed to be collected so that the Singularity Outfit was earned, with further fancy variants unlocked at 95 and 100. This green machine then took on five awesome styles if various helmets were discovered across the map. These were all related to distinguished Outfits from the history of Fortnite, namely Cuddle Team Leader, Drift, Beef Boss, Tomatohead, and Rex. The range of gear with links to famous Outfits got gamers flurrying to progress through the Battle Pass and show off their novel styles.

FACT

The Utopia Challenges were the tasks that needed to be tackled in order to be rewarded with Singularity and her distinguished variants.

SKULL & BOWS

FIND A DARK PLACE AND ECLIPSE THE COMPETITION

SHADOW SKULLY

INTRODUCED IN: SEASON 9
SERIES: SHADOW

Who turned off the lights? No wait, don't panic—Shadow Skully really is all black, with just the beaming white star on her cap and stripes around the bottom of her boots. Part of the Shadows Rising Pack, a limited time offer from the Store that came with two further Outfits, she is the Shadow version of Season 7's Skully and looks totally impressive (and daunting) when teamed up with the Stark Satchel Back Bling. Beware of what lurks in the shadows...

STARK SATCHEL

FACT

The Shadows Rising Pack included seven cosmetics in total: three Outfits, three Back Blings, and a Wrap.

119

SKULL SQUAD
JOLLY TO THE BONE

YULE TROOPER

INTRODUCED IN: CHAPTER 2: SEASON 1
RARITY: EPIC

Skull Trooper retains legendary status in Fortnite, dating back to Season 1 and remaining a mainstay for the biggest streamers. Seeing his Santa-themed buddy make the Item Shop at the end of 2019 was just about the perfect Christmas present players could ask for. Complete with a cute white beard and slightly different boots to Skull Trooper that look more suited to dropping down chimneys, Yule Trooper brings the holiday spirit chilling through your bones.

BRANCH BASHER

FACT

As a Christmas-only Outfit, Yule Trooper is a rare sight in-game and usually can only be snapped up around the festive season. Keep your eyes trained on the Item Shop around the holidays.

SKY STALKER
SURVIVING ON A WING AND A PRAYER

AERONAUT

INTRODUCED IN: SEASON X
RARITY: RARE

If you think of a Battle Royale as embarking on a journey packed with action and adventure, then Aeronaut is an ace addition to your experience. This aviator looks as ready for a twenty-first-century assignment as he would have done eighty years ago, marrying new and old flying styles to perfection. He's the second Outfit from the Sky Stalker set, with the Sky Stalker Outfit making the Item Shop in Season 4. Salute the skies and respect these daredevil navigators.

AERO AXE

SLURP SQUAD

MAKING A MESS IS TO BE EXPECTED

DOUBLE TAP

BIG CHUGGUS

INTRODUCED IN: CHAPTER 2: SEASON 1
RARITY: EPIC

Look at the size of this guy—he's a big ol' warrior! With arms like rocks and tree-trunk legs, Big Chuggus can do some serious damage and if you're ever unsure of what set he's from, he has "slurp" tagged on the chest plate armor. There's greeny-blue liquid pumping to and from his helmet and the eyeballs are full of the stuff, too. Messing with him will not be pretty.

JUGGUS

RIPPLEY VS SLUDGE

INTRODUCED IN:
CHAPTER 2: SEASON 1
RARITY: RARE

Sometimes in Fortnite, you've just got to be prepared to get your hands dirty. Unlocking the messy maverick of Rippley required ticking off Tier 20 of the Battle Pass, but the filthy fun didn't stop there. Sludge, the raging red variant, could then be selected and a special purple dude was achieved after nine missions. There are plenty of colors and character traits on offer, making these highly sought-after Battle Pass Outfits.

SNAKEPIT
RATTLE THE OPPOSITION

SKY SERPENTS

SIDEWINDER

INTRODUCED IN: SEASON 8
RARITY: EPIC

For sure, it's all about the snakes with Sidewinder. The creepy creatures are everywhere, with red snake designs on the shirt, a real-life rattlesnake coiled around the hat... even her eyes look like a viper's! The golden Cobra Back Bling adds another slick touch, as does the Sky Serpents Glider to help you swoop onto the map and hunt down prey.

FACT

There's also an Outfit called Snakepit in the Siege Strike set, which appeared in Season X.

CORRUPTED VOYAGER

INTRODUCED IN: SEASON X
RARITY: EPIC

Get ready for more out-of-this world Outfits from Space Explorers. Funky futuristic suit? Check. Glitchy animated visor? Check. Weird alien-themed Back Bling? Check. There's so much to appreciate here in how Corrupted Voyager looks, plus she has heritage too as an admirable re-skin of Dark Vanguard from Season 3. If she zooms into the Item Shop, don't let her lift off again before you've had a chance to add this Outfit to your locker.

XENOPOD

125

GAMEPLAN

ETERNAL VOYAGER

**INTRODUCED IN: SEASON X
RARITY: EPIC**

Like Moonwalker and Mission Specialist before him in this set, Eternal Voyager featured in the Battle Pass and became unlocked at Tier 87. Looking mean and unpredictable behind that darkened helmet, more unlockable variants could be collected for rising through the Battle Pass and completing missions. The scariest of these was the skull style—even in space this creates an eerie atmosphere!

PIXEL PILOT

FACT

With over twenty different items from five cosmetic categories, if you count the Wrap, Space Explorers is a huge set with so many options!

STANDOUT STYLE
NOT JUST ANOTHER FACE IN THE CROWD

CAMEO VS CHIC

INTRODUCED IN:
CHAPTER 2: SEASON 1
RARITY: EPIC

If you had a time machine and went back to a typical disco in the 1980s, this getup would be a frequent sight on the dance floor. The cropped tiger print top, denim skirt and colored hair of Cameo convey a fun, party-gal look, but make no mistake, this character has a serious side too. Only available through the Battle Pass, the additional Chic style was unlocked when various missions were achieved. Chic is similar in look but her black and pink two-tone outfit suggests that business comes before pleasure for her.

FACT

In addition to Chic, Cameo also had a yellow variation with no flashy sunglasses included, which appeared after nine Overtime Challenges were achieved.

BLADE BAG

READY RUCK

SORANA

INTRODUCED IN:
CHAPTER 2: SEASON 1
RARITY: LEGENDARY

Can you keep a secret? Well, Sorana, a tough-looking female warrior obtained through Chapter 2: Season 1 challenges, also had two covert styles with gray and green pants. These color variants were collected by completing simple hiding missions around the map, giving this Outfit even more desirability. Just make sure you take a shower afterwards if you have to hide in a dumpster....

PARTY
CRASHERS

STAR WALKER
THE LIMITS ARE LIMITLESS

INFINITY

INTRODUCED IN: SEASON X
RARITY: EPIC

Checking out the daily updates in the Item Shop is always cool, and when this Outfit appeared in Season X it sent pulses racing. The figure is incredibly perplexing, consisting of a body that contains flowing and glowing material, a featureless smooth head, and a jacket befitting a mystic time lord. As a true one-off, it reminds gamers that anything is possible amid the Fortnite landscape.

STING

THE BEST PESTS AROUND

BONE WASP

INTRODUCED IN: SEASON X
RARITY: EPIC

One for all the insect lovers out there...
even though Bone Wasp is only a homage
to the flying creature and not a giant-sized
embodiment. This guy is decked out in golden
wasp colors with a relaxing urban spirit and
finished off with a horrifying head that looks
like it's made from either a piece of wood, an
upturned bucket or a leftover pumpkin. You
really don't want to get too close to find out.

**HORNED
STRIKE**

FACT

The Primal Danger Back
Bling is a huge metal
weapon, but it almost
seems a shame to
equip it as it covers the
detailed insect graphic
on the reverse of Bone
Wasp's jacket.

**PRIMAL
DANGER**

STORMLIGHT
SHINING EXAMPLES OF WHAT'S GOOD AND PROPER

LUMI
CORE
GREEN

FLARE

INTRODUCED IN: SEASON 9
RARITY: EPIC

No need to use a searchlight when this pair of bright hipsters are on the scene. Interestingly, the default style is the Outfit with the extra sparkle and jazz compared to the selectable—usually it's the other way round. The default glow style sees Flare's hair, eyes, and sleeve tattoos shine vividly to make this look stand out from the crowd.

MEGABAT

SPLINTERED
LIGHT

NITEBEAM

INTRODUCED IN: SEASON 9
RARITY: EPIC

Luminous energy is the force behind this clean and classic Outfit. Like her male friend, the default Nitebeam boasts bright hair, eyes, and tats, but this time it's pink that rules. Her all-in-one suit is simple and demonstrates her wish to keep things practical and on point around the map.

X-LORD

INTRODUCED IN: SEASON X
RARITY: EPIC

X-Lord is an utterly unforgettable Outfit, looking like a biker-pilot-welder dude with only one thing on his mind—conquering those around him. The cool factor of this cosmetic is ramped up thanks to him only being available in the Battle Pass, as well as the four further unlockable styles included. In all of them the helmet stays on, but the Scavenger style ditches the top to reveal a ripped physique. With his spiked helmet, X-Lord is not an Outfit you want to go head to head with.

TROPHY SACK

FACT

The unlockable Rust variant of X-Lord is based on the popular Rust Lord from the Storm Scavenger set in Season 3.

**FANG
SAWS**

PERFECT PETS

AS LOYAL AND LOVABLE COMPANIONS ON THE ISLAND, YOUR OWN CUTE LITTLE CREATURE IS A PRIZED PART OF FORTNITE

There are far fewer Pets in Fortnite compared to other Items, which makes them very collectible and desirable. These adorable animals can react to changes in a game, make cute sounds, and bring an extra edge to your Back Bling. Check out some of the most precious Pets ever...

DODGER

INTRODUCED IN: SEASON 8
RARITY: EPIC

Foxes are traditionally clever and cunning, and Dodger is a master of, erm, dodging danger and coming along for the ride.

EMPRESS

INTRODUCED IN: SEASON 8
RARITY: EPIC

The crown on the chair shows she's a royal animal, but the purple sunglasses suggest Empress is a fashionable feline too. For many, this is the purr-fect Pet!

WOODSY

INTRODUCED IN: SEASON 8
RARITY: EPIC

Battle Pass players had a big incentive to progress, with Woodsy unlocked at Tier 19 and the selectable Pirate and Gold styles at Tier 38 and 83.

KITSUNE

INTRODUCED IN: SEASON X
RARITY: EPIC

This fox has two tails and looks lovable and scary in equal measure. The Snowstorm and Black variants were unlocked at Battle Pass Tier 45 and 65.

BONESY

INTRODUCED IN: SEASON 6
RARITY: EPIC

A much-loved companion with two selectable Battle Pass styles, Bonesy will always be fondly remembered as Fortnite's first Pet. What a good boy he is!

CAMO

INTRODUCED IN: SEASON 6
RARITY: EPIC

Want a brilliant buddy on the island? Camo the crazy chameleon is a lively little thing strapped to your back, and it will always make you smile.

SCALES

INTRODUCED IN: SEASON 6
RARITY: EPIC

Your scaly sidekick was unlocked at Tier 43 of the Battle Pass. Some say the blue beast is cute, others reckon it's scary... what do you think?

HAMIREZ

INTRODUCED IN: SEASON 7
RARITY: EPIC

Hamirez the hamster comes in tan, pink, or mocha variants and she's an acrobatic animal capable of eye-catching moves around her wheel.

MERRY MUNCHKIN

INTRODUCED IN: SEASON 7
RARITY: EPIC

Part of the 14 Days of Fortnite event, Merry Munchkin was well worth putting the effort in for. Just don't bite off more than you can chew...

REMUS

INTRODUCED IN: SEASON 7
RARITY: EPIC

In grey, skull or ice style, this untamed accomplice has a look that makes opponents stand back. A wild wolf in every sense.

STORM STALKER
DETECTING DISTURBANCES 24/7

STRATUS

INTRODUCED IN: SEASON 9
RARITY: EPIC

Discovering how Stratus worked as a reactive
Outfit was a challenge at first. At a closer
look, though, the mini map technology on his
left arm could be seen detecting the storm
movements and displayed a warning signal.
That was very impressive and very unique,
too. Strap on the Backtracker Back Bling and
that also displayed real-time storm data to
keep you ahead of the game.

BACKTRACKER

TAILWIND TWISTER

RILEY

INTRODUCED IN:
CHAPTER 2: SEASON 1
RARITY: RARE

There's more going on up top here than in the bottom half. The balaclava, cap, and headphones are a busy headwear selection, however it looks fresh and funky accompanying the shiny red jacket and green hoodie. There's little bling and no heavy tech or devices strapped to her arms or legs, meaning Riley is free to concentrate on laying waste to her opponents—while listening to some banging tunes at the same time.

FACT

Riley won a Community Choice vote in Chapter 2: Season 1, meaning it came into the Item Shop on popular demand!

STRIPES AND SOLIDS
RACK 'EM UP

8-BALL VS SCRATCH

INTRODUCED IN:
CHAPTER 2: SEASON 1
RARITY: EPIC

Not only did Chapter 2: Season 1 see the start of an exciting new Fortnite adventure, but Outfits such as this one got players on the edge of their gaming chairs too. Unlockable in the Battle Pass at Tier 60, 8-Ball vs Scratch is totally dominated by his strange pool-ball helmet, with matching white markings on the suit's arms and legs. What's extra awesome about him, though, are the two additional styles of Scratch and Gold. The all-white Scratch even has a corrupted and glitch effect, which begins to take hold past level 100.

BANK SHOTS

CRAZY EIGHT

SUIT UP
DRESS TO IMPRESS

MECH AXE

VENDETTA

INTRODUCED IN: SEASON 9
RARITY: LEGENDARY

Rumors that you need a calculator to keep track of
the number of additional style options for Vendetta
are far-fetched, but he does have plenty to count.
In total there are eleven options for this likeable,
friendly-looking young man in a hooded leather top.
Stage 1 is equipped at Battle Pass Tier 100, with
the hood and top color switching as challenges and
missions are amassed. Attaining XP sees the hood
and mask added, with Vendetta's legs becoming
cyborg to match his mech-like metamorphosis.

RETRIBUTION

SUN SOLDIERS
PRAISE THE RAYS

MEZMER

INTRODUCED IN: SEASON 8
RARITY: RARE

Celebrate the past and the future with this bizarrely enticing costume. This cosmetic features carvings around the face and back of the hands, but there's also a fearsome robot style lurking beneath the hood and jacket. The simple green and black scheme hints at Halloween too. In short, this isn't a character you'd like to meet on a dark night.

HYPNOTIC

AXETEC

SUNBIRD

INTRODUCED IN: SEASON 8
RARITY: RARE

Here you can finally see the bright side of the
Sun Soldiers set as Sunbird is the glowing,
vibrant character that Shadowbird is based
on. Also coming with a selectable no-mask
style, she radiates warmth through her orange
top and vivid headdress. At daybreak this
Outfit will help you fly into action.

SUNRISE

SHADOWBIRD

INTRODUCED IN: SEASON 9
SERIES: SHADOW

Like Shadow Skully, Shadowbird was included in the Shadows Rising Pack as part of a dark and sinister collection of cosmetics. Her bright red lips contrast with the eerie blankness of her vacant white eyes, and the white tips of her ornamental feathers crown the look of a bird wanting to show off her plumage. She's no shy soldier happy to fade into the background, even if she prefers to inflict her damage from the safety of the shadows.

SHADOWBIRD WINGS

BRITE BOARD

BEACH BOMBER

INTRODUCED IN: SEASON 9
RARITY: RARE

Way back in Season 2, Brite Bomber brightened up the map with her unicorn-themed multicolored Outfit. Building on that design, Beach Bomber is prepped for a vacation by the sea and is even bundled with the Brite Board Back Bling, which is an awesome skateboard. Hit the sand with this radiant, sun-loving look.

BRITE BLIMP

BRITE BLASTER

INTRODUCED IN: SEASON X
RARITY: RARE

The mix of black vest and pants with pink and purple neon body warmer and gloves is a nice touch. The spiky-topped bright hair is a winner, too, and the subtle Cuddle Team Leader designs on the reverse of his jacket and single kneepad show that Brite Blaster has a fun side. Equip with the Brite Bashers Back Bling and you'll bring a touch of unicorn to the party, too, as the mythical creature features on one of the handles.

FACT

Beach Bomber was released as part of Fortnite's 14 Days of Summer event, which featured "hot" daily challenges, a new LTM mode, unvaulted weapons, and much more special summer stuff!

SWOLE CAT
A FELINE FORCE CONSTANTLY ON THE PROWL

SKELLEFISH

MEOWSCLES

INTRODUCED IN:
CHAPTER 2: SEASON 2
RARITY: EPIC

This cute creature clearly spends as much time in the gym as he does in Battle Royale. Proud to show off his ripped look as much as his combat skills, Meowscles was a fun choice for any players who picked up the Battle Pass. Just like Brutus, Agent Peely, and most of the secret agent crew, the Ghost and Shadow styles could be selected once challenges were completed. Leaving out just a saucer of milk and a few dried biscuits will not keep this powerful predator purring.

FELINE FUN

SOLID SCRATCH

SYNAPSE

INTRODUCED IN: SEASON 9
RARITY: EPIC

If you see someone sporting the shiny, classy Outfit of Synapse, it's a safe assumption that they had a fun summer of 2019 playing Fortnite. Only featured sparingly at that time in the Item Shop, players needed to be eagle-eyed to snap up this great-looking Outfit that has an air of sportiness, superheroness, and mystiqueness. We're not sure those last two words are actually proper words; however, Synapse is a proper cosmetic in every sense of the word.

HOLO-PACK

TAKARA

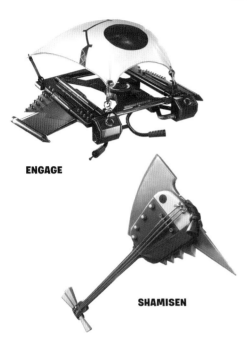

ENGAGE

SHAMISEN

TAKARA

INTRODUCED IN: SEASON 9
RARITY: EPIC

There's something special about Outfits that also share their name with the set name. It's as if it lends them a certain superiority and Takara, from the Takara set (obviously), looks superior... and totally creepy. Her white face with red markings is in keeping with the rest of her costume, and the studs and spikes around the shoulder and neck are a sign of strength and menace. Partner with the monstrous Gaze Back Bling and no-one will dare call you nasty names when facing you in battle!

149

TECH OPS
WE'RE PRETTY SURE THAT'S CHEATING...

ARMATURE

COAXIAL COPTER

CARBON COMMANDO

INTRODUCED IN: SEASON 8
RARITY: RARE

The imposing Carbon Commando was in the PlayStation Plus Celebration Pack 5 and available only as a PlayStation Plus subscriber. This hi-tech soldier is similar in color to Blue Striker, another PS-only character from Season 4, and is a re-skin of the popular Tech Ops in Season 7. The four blue headgear lenses don't actually help in gameplay, but definitely add to the cutting-edge look of this military master.

HYPERNOVA

INTRODUCED IN: SEASON 8
RARITY: RARE

BRUTE FORCE

Those triple lenses on the helmet help place this firmly in the Tech Ops set as Hypernova looks ready for a strike at any time alongside his comrades. His blue-orange jacket camo provides an unusual contrast with the black-orange pants, but not many people will take time out to argue about fashion choices with this fearsome warrior.

DRIVER

BIRDIE

INTRODUCED IN: SEASON 8
RARITY: UNCOMMON

Uncommon Outfits can offer serious value to players looking for something a bit different. When Birdie burst into the Item Shop bringing a big swing of pink and white, it was snapped up by sporty and non-sporty fans alike. There's just her and the Driver Back Bling in the set, but this golf-crazy character looks happy playing solo out on the course, so take control of her and start keeping score.

BASH

INTRODUCED IN: CHAPTER 2: SEASON 1
RARITY: EPIC

If The Leftovers Outfits already look familiar, then don't worry—you're not seeing doubles. The set is made up of Outfits based loosely on existing characters and Bash is a little like Brite Gunner from the Sunshine & Rainbows set. His head is the top part of the Razor Smash Harvesting Tool and with selectable styles known as Hero, Militia, Militia Glow, and Dark, there are plenty of awesome options to get him suited to your preference before dropping from the Battle Bus.

TAKEOUT

RAZOR SMASH

GUACO

INTRODUCED IN: SEASON X
RARITY: RARE

Thanks to a helping of the Beef Boss Outfit from the Durrr Burger set, Guaco serves up a lip-licking look that will make any burrito fan's mouth water. Those eyes are some of the most, er, eye-catching in the entire Item Shop and, dressed like this, players are hungry for eliminations around the island. Just bring the tortilla chips to the party, too.

SNACK ATTACKERS

GUTBOMB

INTRODUCED IN: SEASON X
RARITY: EPIC

Looking like a variant of Beef Boss that's festered for six months, it's clear this guy would do some serious internal damage if anyone dared bite off a piece. He is much less jovial than his Durrr Burger relation and the selectable glow style sees the weird eyes on top of the burger bun come to life. Even the Take Out Back Bling doesn't make this any more luscious on a lunch menu.

HOTHOUSE

INTRODUCED IN: SEASON X
RARITY: EPIC

Rotten tomatoes are another leftover with very little everyday use, although Hothouse looks like he knows how to have some very fruitful forays in Fortnite. Obviously re-skinned from the ever-popular Tomatohead of Pizza Pit fame in Season 3, this character keeps a smiley outlook on life and probably uses his TomCom Back Bling to steer him onto the right path.

RAGSY

INTRODUCED IN: SEASON X
RARITY: EPIC

Cuddle Team Leader can be spotted a mile away, thanks to her bright pink fur and oversized head. From a distance (okay, a very long distance), Ragsy could be confused for the iconic Royale Hearts hero as well, but get closer and you'll soon see the despairing differences. Ragsy is ripped and torn and only half the Outfit that Cuddle Team Leader is... quite literally, as her bottom half is more like a battle-ready soldier than a giant teddy bear.

THE SEVEN
IT'S YOUR LUCKY NUMBER

THE SCIENTIST

INTRODUCED IN: SEASON X
RARITY: LEGENDARY

School science teachers rarely look like this, which is just as well as The Scientist is a hulking beast of a character that doesn't appear as if it wants to teach a bunch of kids anyway. Completing the Meteoric Rise Challenges in the Battle Pass saw this mad mechanical Outfit unleashed, with a white selectable style and four variants available that altered the digital expression on its helmet. A highly covetable Outfit.

FACT

The Visitor is another menacing Outfit from The Seven Set, along with The Scientist, and could be earned by completing all seven challenges from Season 4's Blockbuster Challenges.

THIRD EYE
VISUALIZE THE VICTORY ROYALE

AXIOM

INTRODUCED IN: SEASON 8
RARITY: RARE

Keeping your eye on the enemy is easy when you're dressed as Axiom. This combative dude's triple laser beams are his defining feature and his superhero-esque suit and cool color combo work a treat too. Axiom appears more than capable of covering all of your squad's backs in battle.

DISRUPTOR

PSION

INTRODUCED IN: SEASON 8
RARITY: RARE

Matching up nicely with her male Third Eye buddy, Psion sports the same suit style and has the trio of red laser dots strapped to her head. The Omission Back Bling carries on the jet-like theme and for a final touch of class, equip the set's Disruptor Glider and you'll drop into the island looking like a mean flying machine.

THREE STRIKES
PLAYING HARDBALL

HOME RUN

FASTBALL

INTRODUCED IN: SEASON 8
RARITY: RARE

Bats and balls at the ready, baseball fans. Fortnite has a history of releasing slick sporty Outfits into the Item Shop, and Fastball threw another curveball in Season 8 with her cool orange suit that's perfect for the ballpark. With 'Ballers' emblazoned across her shirt, it's clear this character is a true team player.

SLUGGER

INTRODUCED IN: SEASON 8
RARITY: RARE

Slugging it out on the map is sometimes the only option. That's certainly the case for this Outfit from the Three Strikes set and Slugger looks ready to dig deep and pitch in. The multicolored face paint isn't really necessary; however, it gives him an edge over any opponents he goes head to head with. Batter up, if you dare!

TKO
DELIVERING A KNOCKOUT BLOW

MOXIE

INTRODUCED IN: SEASON X
RARITY: RARE

Part street warrior, part disco dancer and with football-style markings under her eyes, Moxie is a mysterious Outfit full of shimmering colors and textures. She has something going on everywhere you look, from bright shiny leggings to spiky turquoise gloves and shoulder pad to her quirky Moose Back Bling with amusing boxing gloves attached. She's ready for a Battle Royale as soon as the bell rings.

MOOSE

CLOBBER AXE

FACT

Moxie's selectable Dark style tones the color combo down to black and red and sees the character cover her head with a cool hood.

TOY SOLDIER
TOY WITH THE COMPETITION

PLASTIC PATROLLER

INTRODUCED IN: SEASON 9
RARITY: UNCOMMON

This iconic Outfit wouldn't look out of place in the Legendary rarity. Players scrambled to the Item Shop when it first appeared, and whenever it cycled back in, because it's such a simple but effective Outfit. Plastic Patroller looks much more expensive than its Uncommon rating, so grab a bargain here if you can.

TOY TROOPER

INTRODUCED IN: SEASON 9
RARITY: UNCOMMON

Whether in the selectable style of green, gray, or red, Toy Trooper totally took control of the map when she first appeared in Season 9. Her single-tone look comes with just a hint of dirty patches covering her skin, which also proves this toy soldier is battle-hardy to the extreme. Prepare for your mission and march on, soldier!

FACT

Plastic Patroller and Toy Trooper had a small visual update after release, with added mud smears and a brighter outline, to prevent them being too well camouflaged in certain areas of the map.

BANDOLETTE

INTRODUCED IN: SEASON 8
RARITY: RARE

Going for a minimalist style can be a smart move in Fortnite. Bandolette carries nothing but the essentials, with no heavy tech or armor. Those camo pants and flashes of white markings on the skin show that she's suited to hiding out and making a stealthy approach in the hunt for eliminations. Good luck if you're faced with this trooper.

FACT

Bandolier was the first Tropic Troopers Outfit to hit the Item Shop in Season 4, as a muscle-bound dude well capable of taking on an enemy force.

TWIN TURNTABLES
SUPERSTAR DJS

SC3PT3R

MASTER MIX

YOND3R
INTRODUCED IN: SEASON X
RARITY: EPIC

With a stack of style options, this fun re-skin of the awesome DJ Yonder character from Season 6 comes with so many variants you might not be able to choose which to go for. It was a key figure in the Season X Battle Pass, unlocked at Tier 47, so is therefore ultra exclusive. With his helmet on or off, crowned up, or strutting in a green, white, or gold jacket, this music maestro looks majestic while bopping to any tune!

VIVID VISION
KEEP THE COMPETITION IN YOUR SIGHTS

IRIS

INTRODUCED IN: CHAPTER 2: SEASON 2
RARITY: RARE

There are hundreds of fancy, complicated, and tech-inspired Outfits available in Fortnite, but sometimes you just want something clean and crisp with no frills. Coming in the limited time Iris Pack, this Outfit has a default hooded and selectable non-hooded style. The triple-tone sweater with simple circle motif and matching shorts and ankle boots is straightforward and to the point. Enough said, really.

FACT

The Iris Pack came with the Outfit, Roundabout Back Bling, Pop Axe Pickaxe, and 600 V-Bucks. Bargain!

POP AXE

ROUNDABOUT

WESTERN WILDS
THE SHERIFF'S WORST NIGHTMARE

FRONTIER

INTRODUCED IN: SEASON X
RARITY: RARE

Saddle up, partner, and channel your inner cowboy. The previous Western Wilds Outfits of Calamity and Deadfire were progressive and reactive Outfits respectively, but Frontier is a straight-shooting, no-nonsense raider with simple selectable styles that allow you to choose whether he is with or without his dusty brown hat. Strap him up with his Detonator Back Bling for an explosive start when he drops from the Battle Bus.

COVERED CRUSADER

RIO GRANDE

INTRODUCED IN: SEASON X
RARITY: RARE

Another clean and cool Western-themed Outfit with an uncomplicated combination of vest and two-tone brown pants. Rio Grande is a natural riding through deserts, plains, and water basins on her trusty horse and, trust us, she's happy to watch your back in a gun-slinging shootout.

LONGHORN

WHITE TIGER
BIG CATS TAKE DOWN BIG VICTORIES

WILDE

INTRODUCED IN: SEASON 9
RARITY: EPIC

Limited time offer Packs are an amazing value and provide exclusive Outfits and cosmetics. The fashionable Wilde Outfit arrived in the Wilde Pack in Season 9, bundled with the Palette Pack Back Bling and 600 V-Bucks. A mix of animal magic—take a look at that epic white tiger-inspired jacket—and funky summer shorts, with cute spiked pads on the legs, she's a chic customer with a fearsome streak.

FACT

The first Battle Royale limited time Pack was in Season 3 and featured the popular Rogue Agent Outfit.

RUSTLER

INTRODUCED IN: CHAPTER 2: SEASON 1
RARITY: RARE

Rounding up the bad guys and reining in chaos is all in a day's work for this hard-grafting girl. With some crossover to the Western Wilds set—which is all good as cowboys and cowgirls are fine Fortnite favorites—Rustler has the basic tools to get the job done in a no-fuss way. Her red shirt is mirrored in the cool Rustler Plaid Wrap, which gives your weapons and vehicles a wicked Wild West vibe.

LEATHER LUGGER

WRANGLER

INTRODUCED IN:
CHAPTER 2: SEASON 1
RARITY: RARE

Wrangler also carries the cowboy theme, even though the traditional western ranch hat is swapped for a reversed baseball cap. Plenty of players still dig this style, and he looks capable of putting in a shift with the cattle and flexing his power hunting down enemies across the island. The green tinted shades are a nice finishing touch.

WINTER WONDERLAND
AN ICY OPTION TO FREEZE OTHERS IN THEIR TRACKS

SNOWY

TREEFALL

DOLPH

INTRODUCED IN: CHAPTER 2: SEASON 1
RARITY: RARE

This is the best way to sleigh! Dolph is ice cool, masquerading as a chilled-out version of Santa's favorite reindeer while dressed in a cute festive sweatshirt and with tree lights wrapped around his antlers. Weird but wonderful, hey? Match him with the Bough Breaker Back Bling to complete an Outfit that screams holiday happiness from every angle.

BLACK HOLE

ZERO

INTRODUCED IN: CHAPTER 2: SEASON 1
RARITY: LEGENDARY

As the first new Outfit in the Item Shop at the start of Chapter 2: Season 1, this cosmetic was quite a statement, and it was packed with intrigue and mystery thanks to its use of dark and turquoise glowing lights and patterns shifting around its body. Zero's back cosmetic was absolutely stunning and very timely, too—the Black Hole Back Bling represented the very thing that caused the creation of this new dawn in the Fortnite landscape. Zero, we salute you, sir!

DANGER ZONE

INTRODUCED IN: SEASON X
RARITY: RARE

Alongside the release of the Zone Wars Vortex, Downhill River, Desert, and Colosseum LTMs, the Zone Wars Challenge Bundle contained two fierce Outfits. Danger Zone's faded red-to-purple android suit also had a selectable Galaxy Blue variant, which was unleashed after completing style challenges. The Starcrest Shift Back Bling and Hyper Edge Harvesting Tool completed a uniform that was other-worldly to say the least.

HYPER EDGE

HOT ZONE

INTRODUCED IN: SEASON X
RARITY: RARE

Pairing up with Danger Zone was Hot Zone—a dude who really turned up the heat around the map! He, too, came with a cool unlockable mission-based style. Hot Zone was more human than machine, but his face gave no clues away as the hood and mask combo kept his plans under wraps.

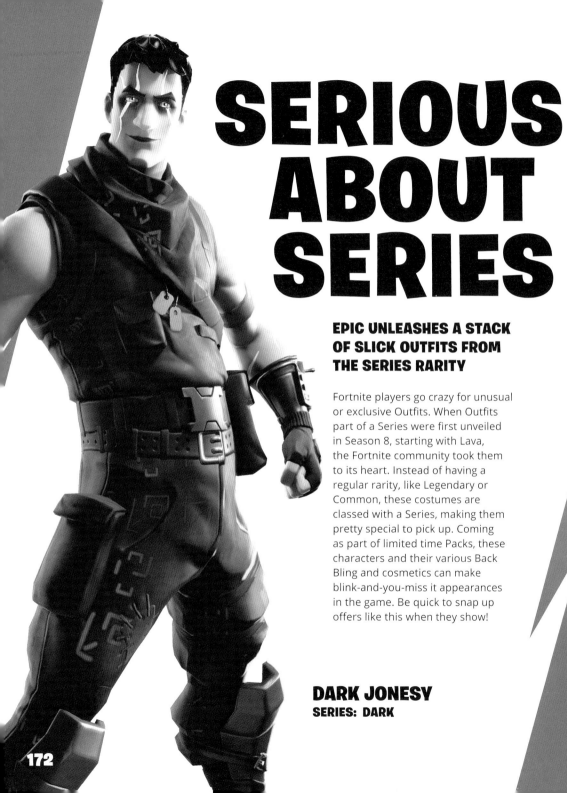

SERIOUS ABOUT SERIES

EPIC UNLEASHES A STACK OF SLICK OUTFITS FROM THE SERIES RARITY

Fortnite players go crazy for unusual or exclusive Outfits. When Outfits part of a Series were first unveiled in Season 8, starting with Lava, the Fortnite community took them to its heart. Instead of having a regular rarity, like Legendary or Common, these costumes are classed with a Series, making them pretty special to pick up. Coming as part of limited time Packs, these characters and their various Back Bling and cosmetics can make blink-and-you-miss it appearances in the game. Be quick to snap up offers like this when they show!

DARK JONESY
SERIES: DARK

DARK RED KNIGHT
SERIES: DARK

FROZEN NOG OPS
SERIES: FROZEN

DARK WILD CARD
SERIES: DARK

THE DEVOURER
SERIES: FROZEN

FROZEN FISHSTICK
SERIES: FROZEN

**MOLTEN
VALKYRIE**
SERIES: LAVA

PERFECT SHADOW
SERIES: SHADOW

SHADOWBIRD
SERIES: SHADOW

**MOLTEN
BATTLE HOUND**
SERIES: LAVA

**SHADOW
SKULLY**
SERIES: SHADOW

Some Series Outfits are special variants of existing Fortnite characters. Remember Skully, from the Skull & Bows set in Season 7? Shadow Skully is a more menacing take on her appearance and Dark Wild Card develops the original Season 5 Wild Card to a more sinister stage. There's often history and a story behind the Series Outfits, although some, like the outrageous The Devourer, just appear from nowhere with frightening impact!

SHADOW STRIKERS
SERIES: SHADOW

MOLTEN CRESTED CAPE
SERIES: LAVA

DARK HATCHLING
SERIES: DARK

MOLTEN ANGULAR SHIFT
SERIES: LAVA

SERIES ACCESSORIES

Some awesome add-ons feature in the Series sets. These include cool Back Bling that make a big impression, like Molten Valkyrie Wings from the Lava Series and the Dark Series' Dark Shield, plus extras like Harvesting Tools, Gliders, Wraps, and even built-in Emotes. Outfits and cosmetics are bundled in each particular pack, offering a great value purchase.

First published in the UK in 2020 by WILDFIRE an imprint of
HEADLINE PUBLISHING GROUP

Cataloguing in Publication Data is available from
the British Library

Hardback 978 14722 7718 3

Design by Amazing15
Printed and bound in Italy by L.E.G.O. S.p.A.
10 9 8 7

HEADLINE PUBLISHING GROUP
An Hachette UK Company
Carmelite House
50 Victoria Embankment
London, EC4 0DZ
www.headline.co.uk www.hachette.co.uk

www.epicgames.com